W9-AWF-677

FAST-FOLDED FLOWERS

Timesaving Techniques for a Quilted Bouquet

LAURA FARSON

To Russ, for understanding me.

©2001 by Laura Farson
All rights reserved.

No portion of this publication may be reproduced or transmitted in any form or by any means, electronic or mechanical, including photocopy, recording, or any information storage and retrieval system, without permission in writing from the publisher, except by a reviewer who may quote brief passages in a critical article or review to be printed in a magazine or newspaper, or electronically transmitted on radio or television.

Published by

krause publications

Please call or write for our free catalog of publications. Our toll-free number to place an order or obtain a free catalog is (800) 258-0929.

Library of Congress Catalog Number: 2001090716
ISBN: 0-87349-253-6

Some products in this book are registered trademarks: Fray Check™, Templar™, Mountain Mist®, Thermore®, Omnigrid®, Dritz®.

Photography by Greg Daniels; illustrations by Laura Farson; and editorial reading by Lynne Beykirch.

The author grants permission to photocopy templates (pages 114 through 127) for personal use in completing the projects in this book.

Preface

I planned to quilt when I retired and got old. Well, I retired once, I am quilting, but I'm not old! Actually, quilting is my job, but I certainly don't consider it work.

As it happens, I began to quilt out of necessity. About ten years ago, the quilt my mom gave me for a wedding gift fell apart after twenty years of daily use. The style was no longer available in stores, and since I had sewn since I could "peddle the treadle," I figured that I could learn to make quilts.

So, I took some classes, bought some books, and went to work.

That quilt and others have long been finished, but I found a real passion.

Since then, I've done some experimenting, and one idea led to another. One of those ideas was to write a book.

This book had a simple beginning with squares. Then came the variations on a square. But when squares were exhausted, I looked at hexagons. Lots of ideas came out of hexagons. Not to be limited, I looked at pentagons and octagons. Triangles slipped in as joining pieces and evolved as a doable shape on their own.

Pentagons proved to be a little too unwieldy and looked more like automobile hood ornaments than quilt blocks, so they're history for now.

Just when I thought all the possibilities were exhausted, another idea came to mind. While traveling through Kansas, I saw some sunflowers and was inspired to experiment with more petals. After some trial and error, my favorite – the twelve-sided sunflower block – grew to fruition.

I hope you like it and many of the other fun flower shapes found in this book.

Table of Contents

So many choices, so little time! And that is exactly why you need the timesaving techniques outlined in this book. Quilt units above made by Laura Farson.

Acknowledgments

I'd like to express my gratitude for many kinds of assistance: those who had confidence in me and gave me opportunities; those who offered advice; friends who listened; people who inspired; and many who went out of their way to help.

Thank you to the companies who gave me generous supplies: American & Efird Inc. for the thread; Northcott Silk Inc., Westfalenstoffe, and Chanteclaire for the fabric; Stearns Technical Textiles Co. for the batting; Clover Needlecraft Inc. for the miniature iron; Dritz Corp. for the rulers; and Pfaff American Sales Corp. for the use of their wonderful sewing machine!

I'm appreciative of the folks at Krause, for giving me this opportunity: Don Gulbrandsen, Paul Kennedy, Debbie Bradley, Jon Stein, and Maria Turner.

Thanks to the quilt shop people: Mary Solomon, Pat Steik, Kathy Jennings, and Lois Weissberg.

And what would I have done without Marian Brockschmidt, Julia Schad, Sue Thompson, and Wilma Fricke, the ladies who loaned me their quilts?

And, of course, I can't forget to thank my quilting buddies, Melania Thompson and Cindy Marshall.

Thank you all for helping me bring this book to life.

Introduction

Among us quilters, there are those who have struggled with curved piecing. My interest was piqued in the early 1970s by the "Cathedral Window" pattern I had saved from a magazine.

It was brought to mind again about five years ago when I saw the pattern in a quilting book.

Fascinated, I bought the book and some fabric from the quilt shop. I made twenty-five blocks and joined them to make a 20-inch square.

It took me weeks!

Since I'm an "immediate gratification" type of person, my thoughts wandered to simpler methods. I began experimenting by sewing two squares of different fabrics together and turning them right sides out. After pressing and folding the corners to the center, I had trouble bending the petal edge.

Cutting the squares on the bias solved that problem.

Intrigued by the possibilities, I began further experiments with other shapes. I made lots of experimental blocks and small projects. Each one led to another with thoughts popping into my head at all hours of the day and night. I took to keeping a notebook with me at all times.

After a while, it occurred to me that I might do some research to see whether this kind of thing had been done before. I combed quilt shops, libraries, and bookstores and bought lots of books and fabric – all in the name of research!

And what fun I've had meeting and discussing this concept with other quilters and sewers.

Since it seemed unique, and I was looking for a career, I decided to write a book on how to make the very same quilts that have brought me so much joy.

There's a rich history of quilt patterns with circles and loops and curves. While looking into the background of curved-pieced quilts, patterns like "Orange Peel" and "Joseph's Coat" came to light. I was daunted by instructions that required cutting 600-plus pieces of part "A" and more than 400 pieces of "B." My future flashed before me – endless curved pieces with no finished projects in sight!

Not one to struggle, however, I've devised a simpler approach.

Fast-Folded Flowers will give you the skills to create beautiful curved-piece quilts without the agony. All techniques are performed with a sewing machine!

The beauty of quilting is that variations on a technique can open up a whole new way of doing things. Quilt types shown at left evolved into some of the methods discussed in this book. Quilts include: "Hearts and Gizzards," owned by Sue Thompson, and three "Cathedral Window" quilts, made by Julia Schad, Wilma Fricke, and Marian Brockschmidt.

The emphasis is on simplicity, but the results look complicated. Curved edges are created when bias folds are turned back in gentle arcs and topstitched.

For the purist, all can be completed easily by hand, although not nearly as quickly.

Twelve different variations are explained in chapters featuring different geometric shapes. Each technique transforms the fabric into a unique petal-accented unit that is joined with others to complete a floral bouquet.

Basic information on terms, techniques, and tools is contained in Chapter One. Many of the terms and techniques are unique to this book, including instructions for: turning back the bias folds to make the petals; cutting fabric pieces with a rotary ruler on a paper template; snipping slashes; binding and borders; the many uses of temporary adhesive; and the insertion of batting within the unit. Review them before proceeding and refer back while making the projects. They are arranged in alphabetical order for easy reference.

The use of photocopied templates that are used as guides for the rotary ruler is recommended. These paper templates are cut out and placed on the fabric with grain line indicators. The rotary ruler is placed over the template and acts as the guide for the rotary cutter.

Temporary adhesive spray is used to secure the templates on fabric while pieces are being cut. It's also used to tack batting in place during the construction.

Batting pieces are cut to fit inside each unit rather than layering after piecing.

Borders are filled with strips of batting to match the thickness with the project.

Patterns and projects are designed to utilize the greatest amount of fabric based on 40- to 45-inch widths. Although some of the cutting produces "waste," it is easily recycled into other projects.

Pieces are sized to match standard rotary rulers.

Chapters Two through Six contain instructions on different shapes, beginning with squares and triangles and progressing to hexagons and octagons. The largest is the dodecagon with twelve sides, more descriptively known as a "sunflower."

Within each chapter is the basic technique in which two shapes are cut from fabric, i.e. two squares or two stars. These are placed right sides together and sewn. A piece of batting is fused onto the inside surface, and the unit is flipped right-side out. Corners are folded to the center making flaps – and voila! – the block is ready to be joined to others like it. Once a group is joined, the folded flaps are turned back and topstitched to form lovely lined petal areas.

Once you have mastered the basic technique, the instructions move on to enhanced versions of each shape.

The second version is the accented-petal variation. Those petal areas that are turned back

Create the effect of a "Joseph's Coat" style in half the time and without sacrificing the quality of the resulting quilt. The block at left was made by Laura Farson, 2001.

are lined with an accent fabric that makes a curved outline. Instructions for this technique are given for squares, hexagons, and octagons. Triangles are sewn onto the center fabric cut into a square, hexagon, or octagon, forming a star. These "stars" are placed right sides together with a back piece and are then sewn. After a cutout piece of batting is fused onto the inside surface, the unit is flipped to the right side and pressed flat. Points or corners are folded to the center forming flaps. The unit is ready to be joined with others like it.

Once a group is made, simply opening the flaps of touching units and sewing in the folds completes the joining. For hexagons and octagons, filler pieces are made using simple templates and joined in the open areas between units.

Two special variations are possible with squares. The simplest is the "Cutaway Square" variation. Using a template, the curved areas of the petal flaps are cut before construction. Once the units are sewn and folded, the petal flaps are already formed in an arc without the folded edge.

The "Petals and Ribbon" variation, featured in the background of the cover, is made by sewing accent strips onto four triangles. These pieces are inserted between the inside and outside fabric layers, and when folded, form the crossed accent stripes. The folded triangle edges are turned back to form petals. The whole looks like wrapped packages.

Each chapter features one or more projects for each technique. There is a full range of easy, intermediate, and advanced selections. Many variations in size and color are possible.

For any of the projects, be sure to select a group of fabrics that coordinate. Read through the instructions and construct a "sample" block or two. Such samples work wonderfully as hot pads when joined back to back. Or leave one end open on a pair and slip a tile into the pocket for a table trivet!

After completing some sample blocks by following the chapter instructions, begin with "Country Petals" or "Raggedy Edges," both easy projects to make.

Browse through the chapters and make a four-unit project such as "Peachy Petals" or "In the Pink."

Try a color study by making the three "Dreaming In Flowers" variations. A larger project, such as "Petals in the Ferns" has just twelve units.

For gift-giving, make the "Turkish Bazaar" or "Navy Blues" for pillows. Consider "Holly Berries" as a perfect gift for the holidays.

There are so many possibilities.

Have fun…play…enjoy!

basic information

Many of the techniques in Fast-Folded Flowers *are unique. They are described and illustrated in this chapter. It's worthwhile to review them before embarking on a project.*

I encourage you to make practice blocks. Not only will you build and refine your skills, you'll also produce a collection of handy mats to use!

In this chapter, you will also find definitions of terms and descriptions of tools. Some of the information will be review, but many items are special. They are organized in alphabetical order to make it easier for later reference.

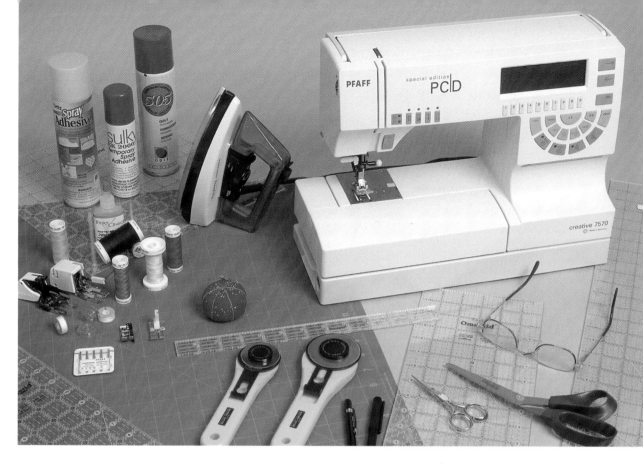

Accessories

Needed tools and accessories include:

- an iron
- silk and flat-headed pins
- a medium (45 millimeter) and a large (60 millimeter) rotary cutter
- eye glasses
- pencils and permanent pens
- rotary rulers with ¼-inch, 60-degree, and 45-degree markings
- spare sewing machine needles
- bobbins
- thread
- ¼-inch foot for the sewing machine
- small 4-inch scissors and large sewing shears
- rotary cutting mat
- Fray Check™
- sewing machine
- a walking foot for the sewing machine.

Unique uses of these tools are discussed in the listing of the specific tool.

Adhesive/Basting

Temporary spray adhesive is used to "baste" batting to the inside fabric prior to turning a unit to the right side. It is also useful when applied to the backside of paper templates prior to cutting the fabric pieces of quilts.

Remember: Use spray adhesive in a well-ventilated area and avoid breathing the spray. Be sure to read the manufacturer's instructions.

1. Place the piece to be sprayed, usually the template or batting, in a shallow cardboard box.
2. Spray lightly and evenly over its surface.
3. Position the batting or template in place.
4. The piece can be repositioned for a few minutes. Most temporary adhesives dissipate quickly.

1.1 There are various types of batting on the market. Use the lightest and thinnest for these projects.

1.2 Batting is easily cut, using a ruler, template, and rotary cutter.

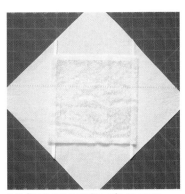

1.3 For best results, place your batting in the center of the block.

1.4 For star-based units, the batting should be centered.

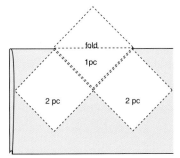

1.5 Follow this cutting diagram when working with a 1-yard piece of fabric.

1.6 Use the line to guide you as you sew.

Batting

Batting is the layer of insulation and sometimes stiffening material placed between the front and back layers of a quilt. It can be cotton, wool, or polyester. The lightest and thinnest batting works best in flower units. (See 1.1)

Inserting batting is easy in flower units. A same-shaped piece is cut to fit within the inner boundary of the folded unit.

Fusible batting is especially desirable in the units that are turned right-side out through a slash.

Non-fusible batting can be temporarily attached using a spray adhesive.

Batting can be cut using a template, ruler, and rotary cutter. (See 1.2)

1. For square units, fold the batting onto itself to create four layers.
2. Cut a strip of batting the width of the square.
3. Crosscut the strip into squares.
4. Place the piece of batting in the center of the block according to the project instructions. (See 1.3) For star-based units, the batting is centered with equal space around all sides. (See 1.4)

Bias

Bias is the diagonal of the fabric grain. It has "give" and is very useful in your projects when turning back petals.

To facilitate the turning on square units, components of the unit are cut on the bias. Most commonly, 12½-inch squares are cut. At left is a cutting diagram to illustrate how to place the ruler on a 1-yard piece of fabric. (See 1.5)

Binding

A single layer of fabric is used for binding the projects. The step-by-step process is described in the following sequence of pictures and illustrations:

1. To find the number of strips needed, measure the total distance around the project, add them together plus 24 inches for joining the strips together and for turning the corners.
2. Once the total length of binding fabric is determined, divide that total by 40 inches (the net width of most fabrics).
3. Round up to the next whole number. This is the number of 40-inch strips needed.
4. Multiply this number by the width of the binding strip.

Usually, the projects in this book have a 1¾- or 2-inch strip. For example, if a project requires six strips, multiply six by 1½ inches for a total of 9 inches. You will need 9 inches of binding fabric.

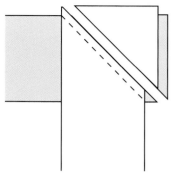

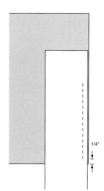

1.7 Trim away the fabric, leaving an ⅛-inch seam allowance.

1.8 Press the seam allowance open.

1.9 Sew along the raw edges to exactly ¼-inch from the corner.

Binding continued

5. Join the binding strips by placing the ends right sides together at a right angle ¼-inch in from the crossed pieces. Mark a line diagonally from the upper left intersection to the lower right intersection.
6. Sew along the line as indicated in the photo. (See 1.6)
7. Trim away the fabric, leaving an ⅛-inch seam allowance. (See 1.7)
8. Press the seam allowance open. (See 1.8)
9. Place a binding strip right-side down along the raw edge of the joined units of the project. Place it at least 6 inches from any corner. Leave a 6-inch tail of unsewn strip to be used for joining.
10. Sew along the raw edges to exactly ¼-inch from the corner. (See 1.9)
11. Fold the binding strip open at a 45-degree angle. The right side of the binding strip will be facing up. (See 1.10)
12. Refold the strip upon itself so that it turns the corner. The binding strip will be face down on the corner folds. (See 1.11)
13. Sew the next side of the project.
14. Repeat the sewing steps for each corner.
15. On the last side, leave 3 inches unsewn and a tail of binding strip. Lay the two loose pieces of binding strip along the raw edge until they meet in the center of the unsewn area.
16. Bend them back on each other and finger-press.
17. Join the two ends of the binding strip by placing them right sides together, and sewing the finger-pressed fold.
18. Trim the extra binding fabric.
19. Press the seam open.
20. Sew the joined binding strip onto the project.
21. Turn the binding right-side out and press open.
22. Turn the project to the backside, and fold the binding fabric onto itself so that the raw edge just touches the raw edge of the project.
23. At the corners, tuck the raw edge of the binding into the corner. (This may take a little fussing.)
24. Fold the binding again so that it's folded edge covers the stitching line on the back of the project.
25. At the corners, fold one side first and then the second side over the first, making a 45-degree fold.
26. Pin the binding. (See 1.12)
27. Topstitch either on the front or the backside of the project. When topstitching on the front, be sure that the folded binding is caught in the stitching.

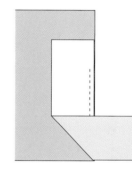

1.10 Fold the binding strip open at a 45-degree angle.

1.11 Refold the strip upon itself so that it turns the corner.

1.12 Pin the binding and topstitch.

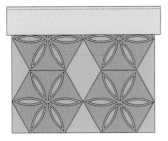

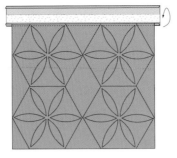

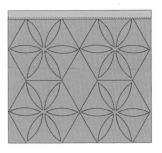

1.13 Place the first border strip right-side down on the long side of the project. Sew.

1.14 Turn a ¼-inch seam allowance along the raw edge of the border strip.

1.15 Trim the border pieces even with the project.

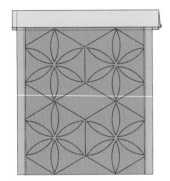

1.16 Fold the border strip back onto itself, right sides together, lining up the folded seam allowance with the sewn seam allowance.

1.17 Stitch across both folded corners, trim the seam allowance, clip across the corners, and fuse batting strip between the seamed ends of the border strip.

Border

Borders are the frames around the outside of a project. Because they are finished on the outside edges, the addition of binding is not needed. The borders in this book are folded over a strip of batting to create a thickness that matches the depth of the units. Project instructions specify the width of a border strip.

1. To change the width of a border, cut the border strip at double the width of the desired finished border plus ½-inch. For example, you would cut strips 6½ inches wide for a 3-inch finished border.

2. Cut the batting filler strips ¼- to ½-inch narrower than the finished width (or 2½ to 2¾ inches for the 3-inch finished border described previously).

3. The length of two border strips is the same as two sides of the project. For a rectangular project, sew the longer sides first. The border looks more balanced with the other sides overlapping the first border strips. The length of the other sides is the distance along the remaining side of the project plus two times the finished width of the added border strips. (In the case of the 3-inch finished border, this would be 7½ inches – 6 inches plus 1½ inches – for a seam allowance long enough for trimming.)

4. Place the first border strip right-side down on the long side of the project, and sew. (See 1.13)

5. Press the border strip open and turn the project to the backside. (See 1.14)

6. Turn a ¼-inch seam allowance along the raw edge of the border strip.

7. Lay a strip of batting against the raw edge of the project. Spray or press-fuse the batting.

8. Fold the fold over the batting, covering the stitching line. Sew along the folded edge. Repeat for the opposite side.

9. Trim the border pieces even with the project. (See 1.15)

10. Turn the project over.

11. On the front side of the project, center the right side of the border strip along the raw edge of the project, across the first two border strips. Sew along the raw edge.

12. Press the border strip open.

13. Turn a ¼-inch seam allowance along the raw edge of the border strip.

14. Fold the border strip back onto itself, right sides together, lining up the folded seam allowance with the sewn seam allowance. (See 1.16)

15. Stitch across the folded corners so that the stitching is just outside the finished edge of the first border piece. (See 1.17)

16. Trim the seam allowance to approximately ⅛-inch and clip across the corners. (See 1.17)

17. Spray-fuse or press-fuse a 2¾-inch-wide strip of batting cut to fit flat between the seamed ends of the border strip. (See 1.17)

18. Turn the border piece right-side out. Smooth the batting inside the border.

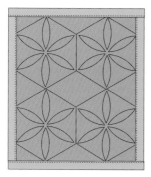

1.18 Turn the border piece right-side out and smooth the batting inside. Press and stitch along the folded seam. Repeat for other side.

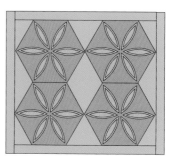

1.19 To the second two border strips, sew a 3- by 4½-inch strip of outer fabric across each end. This end strip forms the corner.

Border continued

19. Press and stitch along the folded seam allowance. (See 1.18)

20. Repeat for the remaining side to complete the process. (See 1.20)

Borders With Corner Blocks

1. For borders with contrasting or coordinating corners, as in "Country Petals" on pages 26 and 27, cut a border strip from each color with the inner color 2 inches wide.

2. Cut the outer color 3 inches wide.

3. Cut two more inner and outer strips ½-inch plus the length of the other two sides.

4. With right sides together, sew an inner color strip to an outer color strip of the same length. You will have a 4½-inch-wide striped border strip.

5. Repeat for the other three two-color strips.

6. To the second two border strips, sew a 3- by 4½-inch strip of outer fabric across each end. This end strip forms the corner. (See 1.19)

When attaching the border strips to the project, place the inner fabric of the first two strips along the raw edge to be sewn. Continue with the border instructions.

When attaching the second (and following) pieced border strips, match the joints of the inner and outer border with the joints of the border corner pieces. (Refer to the picture of "Country Petals" in Chapter Two, page 27.)

Chain-Piecing

Chain-piecing is an efficient way to sew similar pieces. It consists of feeding similar pieces, one right after the other, through the sewing machine without cutting the thread between each piece.

1. Sew a first piece.

2. Follow with a second similar piece at the presser foot. Sew the second piece.

3. Continue placing pieces through the sewing machine without cutting the thread.

4. When you have finished a group, cut the thread at the end and in between each piece.

Cutting

Fabric is cut using a rotary cutter and ruler on a self-healing mat, with paper templates for guides. Project instructions will indicate how the fabric is to be folded.

For triangle-, hexagon-, and octagon-shaped pieces, most frequently the fabric will be folded matching the selvedge and then folded again matching the fold

1.20 When completed, your project with borders will look like this.

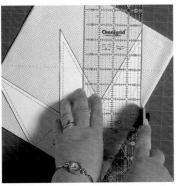

1.21 Place a clear-lined rotary ruler on the template, hold the ruler in place with your non-cutting hand, and cut with a rotary cutter.

Helpful Hint

◆◆◆

When preparing fabrics, wash dark colors together and rinse at least twice. It's worth the time upfront to check for colorfastness.

1.22 For simple joining, open the adjacent flaps, match the fold lines, and sew in the fold.

Cutting continued

to the selvedge. This creates four layers and four pieces at a time when cut.

It's advisable to use the largest-diameter rotary cutter (60 millimeters) in this instance. A sharp blade is a must!

1. Place the paper template on the fabric, matching the grain line.
2. Place a clear-lined rotary ruler on the template so that the ¼-inch line of the ruler is directly on top of the ¼-inch line of the template. (See 1.21)
3. With your non-cutting hand, hold the ruler in place and then cut along the ruler with the rotary cutter. (See 1.21)

Dual-Feed

A built-in sewing machine feature that advances both the top and bottom layers of fabric. (Also see "Walking Foot," page 21.)

Fabric Preparation

Cotton fabric should be washed, dried, and pressed before cutting. Laundering should mimic the method you will use when the project is complete. (See Helpful Hint at left)

Fabric measurements for projects are rounded to the next-highest ¼- or ⅓-yard. The given yardage assumes that uneven edges have been removed.

Grain Line

The grain line of fabric runs parallel to the selvedge. The straight of grain is both parallel and at right angles to the selvedge. Many templates are marked with a designated grain line. Place the line of the template in the same direction as the fabric's straight of grain.

Joining

Completed units are joined by several methods. The simplest is to open the adjacent flaps, match the fold lines, and sew in the fold. This works for square, triangular, and hexagonal units. (See 1.22)

Join longer rows of units together first. Instructions for projects give specific joining plans.

Some topstitching of petals can be done through the middle of long rows before the rows are joined. These narrower strips are easier to manage in the sewing machine.

In projects where many flaps converge creating a space, a filler piece, which resembles a small pillow, is made to fit the space. Specific instructions for making filler pieces are included in the chapters and with the project instructions.

On the backside of the project, a filler piece is placed over the space between units. The edges of filler pieces are thinner so that the bulk falls into the space rather than in the seamed area. The corners are lined up, and the piece is pinned or taped into place.

On the front side, the flaps over the filler pieces are opened and pinned into place. Sewing through the folds of the flaps and the filler pieces joins the pieces. (See photo 6.16 on page 107 of Chapter Six.)

Petals

Petals are created when a folded flap of fabric is turned back on itself. The edge of the fabric layer is on the bias providing ease to the turning process. The turning takes place as you topstitch the petal in place. (See "Turning Back Petals," page 20.)

Quilting

Quilting may be desirable on the simpler projects such as two- or three-color squares. Shadow, or outline, quilting is quite lovely as it accentuates the petal effects and is easy to execute. Random meandering also works well as it puffs up the petal areas.

Rotary Cutter

A rotary cutter is a fabric-cutting tool that resembles a pizza cutter. It is placed against a plastic ruler, which acts as the guide, and rolled through a layer of fabric that is lying on a rotary mat. The blade slices the fabric in a straight line.

Rotary Mat

The rotary mat is made of a material that resists cutting and serves to protect the surface it covers from being cut by the rotary blade.

Rotary Ruler

Transparent rulers are the guides used to cut parts of the projects in this book. I find the most useful rulers to have increments of $\frac{1}{8}$-inch and 30-, 45-, and 60-degree lines.

Seam Allowance

Seam allowances are always $\frac{1}{4}$-inch unless otherwise stated. Quite often the seam allowance will be trimmed to $\frac{1}{8}$-inch. However, don't be tempted to change the seam allowance. They are specifically designed for successful construction. When sewing on the bias, the $\frac{1}{4}$-inch gives some leeway.

Helpful Hint

◆◆◆

When slashing, most star blocks are bias on every other petal flap. On the triangle unit, the hexagon piece has bias on alternating edges.

1.23 Create the slash by first pinching one layer of fabric and making a small clip across the pinch with the scissors.

1.24 Insert the scissors and cut across the bias for about 2 inches.

Sewing Machine

All stitching is done on a sewing machine. It is very helpful to have the ability to change stitch length.

Slash

The slash is used to turn a unit right-side out without having to sew up a seam allowance. Slashes should always be bias cut and should never be cut along the grain line; the latter will cause fraying.

It is also important to put the slash in a place that won't be seen and will be sealed inside a petal. Slash locations are indicated in the chapter illustrations. Place a slash under the area of a flap that will be folded completely over the slash after the petals are turned.

On star-shaped units, the slash can be cut in the central area of the inner petal fabric. Plan the location of the slash so that it can easily be cut on the bias. (See Helpful Hint at left)

1. Create the slash by first pinching one layer of fabric and making a small clip across the pinch with the scissors. (See 1.23)
2. Insert the scissors and cut across the bias for about 2 inches. (See 1.24)

When cutting a slash in a star-shaped piece, avoid cutting in the pointed area. Cut in the central part away from the fold. It is helpful to fold in one of the points to check which area will be covered when the unit is complete.

Spray-Basting

Batting is sprayed with temporary adhesive and placed on the inside fabric of a unit prior to turning the unit right-side out. The temporary adhesive keeps the batting in place while turning the units. It is also used to tack units in place prior to topstitching to the front of pillows. (Also see "Adhesive," page 11.)

Stitch Length

Set your stitch length at ten to twelve stitches per inch. The 2.5-millimeter setting on the newer computerized machines is fine. It is short enough to be secure but long enough to remove when necessary!

In areas that are later trimmed – such as the inside and outside corners of units – a shorter stitch length is preferred. As you sew the two layers together, reduce the stitch-length setting about ½-inch from the corner. (For manual machines fifteen to twenty stitches per inch would be recommended. Computer models read 1.5 millimeters.)

Strip

A strip is a piece of fabric cut from selvedge to selvedge. It is assumed to be 40 inches of usable fabric after shrinkage and removal of the selvedge edge.

Templates

The preferred method of making templates is to make photocopies and cut them out, rather than tracing onto plastic. Since all templates in this book (but one) consist of straight lines, I find it easier to cut fabric by using a rotary ruler placed over the paper template.

Line up the ruler's ¼-inch line on the dotted line of the template. The ruler acts as the guide for the rotary cutter, and the template remains under the ruler.

Full-size templates are located in the back section of the book. They are labeled and referenced in appropriate chapters or projects. Make the number of photocopies of templates required for the desired project. Cut on the solid lines.

When diamond-shaped pieces are joined to make a larger template, use your ruled rotary mat to line the pieces up before taping them together.

For a hexagon, three pieces make a straight line across the middle.

Four pieces of an octagon will be half the template.

Instructions for the dodecagon are given in Chapter Six, pages 102 to 107.

When instructed, cut an additional copy (or copies) of the template inside the dotted seam line for a batting template. (See Helpful Hint, top right)

Triangles

Corner and side triangles are used to fill in the sides of projects to make them "square." Instructions for their construction are included within the relevant chapters.

Trimming/Clipping

1. Trim straight sides of units by placing the rotary ruler along the seam line with the ⅛-inch line along the stitching.
2. Roll the rotary cutter along the edge of the ruler, cutting away the approximate ⅛-inch edge. (See 1.25)
3. At the corner of a square or the point of a star-shaped piece, cut the fabric at an angle in toward the point using a scissors.
4. Trim off the tip of the small point. Be careful to leave three or four threads outside the stitch line. (See Helpful Hint, bottom right)
5. At inside corners, while leaving a few threads uncut, clip straight into the corner with scissors.
6. Trim the seam allowance at an angle toward the clip.

Helpful Hint

♦♦♦

Photocopy batting templates on colored paper and mark as needed to avoid miscuts.

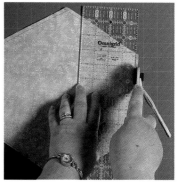

1.25 Roll the rotary cutter along the edge of the ruler, cutting away the ⅛-inch edge.

Helpful Hint

♦♦♦

When trimming or clipping, apply a very small amount of Fray Check liquid to the point.

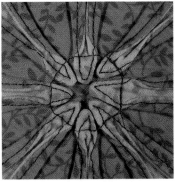

1.26 Pin the center corners or points. If desired, baste the points with machine stitching.

1.27 Sew over the folded fabric for about an inch.

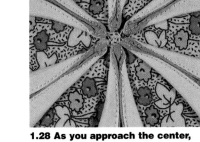

1.28 As you approach the center, return the fabric to the flat position and anchor the last area with three or four topstitches.

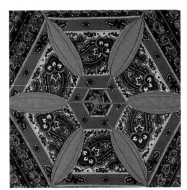

1.29 The petal area can be turned back to accentuate a "fussy-cut" design.

Turning Back Petals

1. Prepare to turn back the petals by pinning the center corners or points. If desired, baste the points with machine stitching. (See 1.26)
2. Pin the flaps in the middle area as well as near the corners and points to keep them from shifting during the topstitching process.
3. Begin at the corner or middle of a unit. Set the sewing machine needle through all the fabric layers at the center point or at the corner of the folded flap.
4. With the flap flat, take three or four stitches.
5. Leave the needle in the fabric and raise the presser foot. (A "needle-down" function is useful here.)
6. Fold the bias edge of the fabric back onto itself in a gentle arc.
7. Lower the presser foot, and sew over the folded fabric for about an inch. (See 1.27)
8. With the needle in the fabric, raise the presser foot and adjust the direction of the sewing and the arc of the folded fabric. The arc of the folded fabric will naturally be thinner at the corner, wider in the middle, and taper at the end.
9. Lower the presser foot, and continue sewing along the edge of the folded fabric.
10. When nearing the end of the folded flap, return the fabric to the flat position and anchor the last area with three or four topstitches. (See 1.28)
11. With the needle in the fabric, raise the presser foot and turn back along the other side of the petal flap.

You may wish to topstitch more and turn back less, depending on the pattern formed by the fabric. As you can see in the "fussy-cut" border fabric at right, the petal edges are neatly outlined by the stripes. (See 1.29)

Turning Right-Side Out

Once the slash is made (see "Slash" on page 18 for instructions), gently pull the fabric through the hole from the inside.

For star-shaped pieces, after the center area is flipped, pull the star points out of their "pockets" by gently grabbing the fabric inside the little tunnel and pulling it out.

The next section explains how to finish the points.

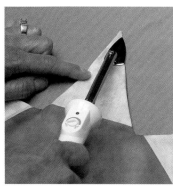
1.30 Use a miniature iron to assist with pressing the points flat.

Turning Out Corners and Points

Fully turn points by pulling the fabric to the surface with a pin. This takes a bit of practice. Avoid pulling the threads individually as they can pull out of the stitching. (If the trimming was too close to the stitching, this can easily happen.)

If your seam allowance shrunk to less than ⅛-inch, spread a little Fray Check with a toothpick along the cut edges of the thread before you turn the unit.

Press the points flat, making sure the seam allowances are fully open. A mini-iron is ideal for this step. (See 1.30)

Unit

The term "unit" refers to an individual part of a project.

Contrary to the term "block" used in the traditional quilting sense, a unit has a front and a back and often batting within.

Parts of units are described at the beginning of each chapter.

Walking Foot

A walking foot is a sewing machine attachment that advances both the lower and upper fabrics through the sewing machine. Its use is especially helpful when sewing across the bias of fabric. The seams lie flatter because the fabrics are even.

Sewing machines with a built in dual-feed feature function in the same manner as a walking foot but with greater visibility and ease of use.

Work Area Organization

Convenience is the key to organizing your workspace.

Place your sewing machine close to the ironing board. The more your sewing work is pressed between steps, the better the results.

Place a rotary mat next to your sewing machine. Many sizes are available; or if you have an old one, cut it to fit the workspace available.

2 squares

quares are simple, quick, and easy. Choose from many different fabric types. Many successful squares can be made from traditional quilt cottons, homespuns, loose weaves, and flannels.

"Glowing Embers" is an example of accented petal squares. This quilt was made by the author, who says this color combination isn't for everyone, but it does exemplify her wild side.

Basic Squares

The basic square is made from an inside and an outside fabric. The outside fabric is folded so that it forms the backside of the project and the front area that surrounds the petals. The inside fabric only shows inside the petal area. Some measure of contrast is desirable, and lots of contrast can be fun!

If you want an all-over pattern, choose two fabrics – one for the inside and one for the outside. The "Country Petals" project (page 27) is made this way.

More variety is possible by changing just the inside fabrics. "Batik Watercolor" (page 29) has many flower colors with just one outside fabric. It's a good example of a low-contrast combination.

Notice how much more the petal effects stand out in "Country Petals."

Helpful Hint

◆◆◆

For a first project, cutting these squares on point (with bias edges) is recommended. This method requires more fabric with leftover triangle-shaped pieces; they may be recycled as parts for other projects in later chapters. (Refer to "Bias," page 12.)

Helpful Hint

◆◆◆

To make step 5 easier, lift a single layer of fabric at about the center of where you would like the slash. Pinch it into a tiny fold and snip across the fold. (Be sure you have only one layer of fabric!) Insert your scissors and snip, cutting 1 inch first in one direction and then an inch in the opposite. Remember that cutting across the bias keeps the slash from fraying.

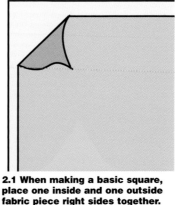

2.1 When making a basic square, place one inside and one outside fabric piece right sides together.

2.2 With the inner fabric facing up, cut a slash 2 inches wide through just one layer of fabric.

Traditional instructions

1. For the neat and tidy version of the basic square, start by cutting equal numbers of 12½-inch squares from the inside and outside fabrics. (See Helpful Hint, top left)
2. Place one of the inside and one of the outside fabric pieces right sides together. (See 2.1)
3. Pin at the corners and sew all four sides with a ¼-inch seam allowance.
4. Trim the seam allowance to ⅛-inch using a ruler and rotary cutter. Snip across the corners to smooth them.
5. With the inner fabric facing up, cut a slash 2 inches long through **just one layer**, across the bias in one of the corners about 1½ inches from the corner. (See 2.2 and the Helpful Hint)

Batting

The very lightest and thinnest works best. (Mountain Mist's® "Goldfuse"or "Quilt Light," or Thermore® by Hobbs.)

Use a medium-hot iron; too much heat can melt the batting.

1. If batting is required or desired, cut 8-inch squares of batting.
2. To position the batting, fold the fabric square in half in both directions, and finger-press the center points along the sides.
3. Line up the corners of the batting pieces with the center finger-pressed folds. Note that the batting square sits diagonally on the square just inside the dotted line shown in the illustration. (See 2.3)
4. Spray-fuse or press-fuse to the wrong side of the outside fabric. (See the "Basting" and "Batting" sections, pages 11 and 12.)
5. Turn the piece right-side out by gently pulling the fabric from the inside through the slash. Pay special attention to the corners so that all the fabric is turned to the seam allowance.
6. Press the square flat, making sure the seam allowances are fully open.
7. Fold the square in half, and finger-press a crease in the center. Fold in the opposite direction, and crease again to form a cross in the center of the square.
8. Open the square, and fold the four corners to the center crease forming a smaller square.
9. Press the folds by setting the iron on the folds. Be careful: Smearing the iron over the folded piece will cause distortion. (See 2.3)
10. Prepare the remaining square units in the same manner.
11. Once the squares are complete, arrange them as shown in the project or in your own pattern.

Joining

The units are sewn together in rows.

1. Open the flaps of two touching squares, match the folds.

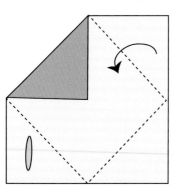

2.3 Press the folds by setting the iron on the folds. Be careful: Smearing the iron over the folded piece will cause distortion.

2. Pin together, and sew in the fold. (See 2.4)
3. Fold the flaps back to their respective units.
4. Press again to set the seams and pin the flaps in the center.
5. Once all the rows are joined, line up two rows side by side.
6. Open the row of flaps on both sections.
7. Match the joints and the adjacent fold lines.
8. Pin across the folds.
9. Sew the two rows together by stitching in the fold.
10. Press the flaps back to their original unit, press, and pin the centers.
11. Repeat with the remaining rows.

Binding

1. Bind the outside edges of the project with a single layer of fabric. (See "Binding" on page 12 of Chapter One for photos and illustrations.)
2. After completing the binding, finish topstitching the petals.
3. Turn back the petals and topstitch by machine or a hand-sewn method.
4. Begin at the center or a corner of a square. Place three to four stitches in the flap before turning it back to reveal the inner fabric.
5. With the sewing machine needle in the fabric, raise the presser foot and turn back the bias edge.
6. Lower the presser foot, and sew along the edge of the turned-back flap.
7. As you approach the center or outside corner, return the flap to its original unturned position and topstitch for three to four stitches. This forms a flat center and flat outside corner.
8. Repeat this process without stopping by crossing over the corners and centers to turn back all the flaps. (See 2.5)

Raggedy Edges Version

It's simple with frayed edges! Use this for a group craft project. It has minimal sewing steps and will build confidence in new sewers.

Choose loose woven homespun or flannel fabric and don't wash or dry it. Plaids and prints look great when matched with a plain cream or other neutral for the inside.

1. Cut the 12½-inch squares as before, but they **must** be on the bias.
2. Place one inside square on an outside square, right sides out.
3. Find the center by alternately folding to the center and finger-pressing.
4. Fold all four of the two-layered corners to the center. Press the folds.
5. Or, cut an 8¼-inch square of heat resistant Templar® plastic and place it on the diagonal of the two layered squares.
6. Press the corners to the center of the plastic guide square.
7. Remove the Templar-square, and insert the batting.
8. Cut 8-inch squares of batting. This seems too small, but the bulk of the two fabric squares "eats up" some of the fabric in the folding.
9. Insert a square of batting between the layers of the folded squares. The batting will be set on the diagonal.
10. Arrange the squares according to the project or your plan.
11. Join the squares by opening the touching flaps and sewing on the fold line. Be careful not to rearrange the two layers of fabric and batting.
12. Once all the squares are joined, fold back the raw bias edges into petal shapes.
13. Like the traditional method, sew three to four stitches before turning back the petal. Finish by flattening the petal fabric for three to four stitches from the end.
14. Bind the same way as in the traditional method.
15. Throw the project in the washer and dryer for soft and fluffy edges!

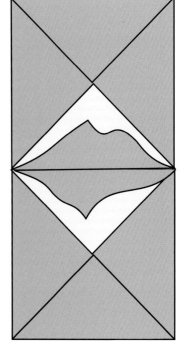

2.4 Open the flaps of two touching squares, match the folds, pin together, and sew in the fold.

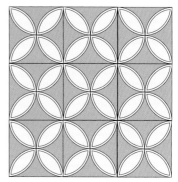

2.5 A completed basic square design, with units repeated and bound together, will look like the above illustration.

Country Petals
Basic Square

Finished size: 28 inches square
Difficulty level: Easy
Block size: 8-inch squares

Rich, deep burgundy and green give this quilt a homey country feel. Perk it up with a spring palette of yellow and white flowers. Or go old-fashioned with scrappy grandmotherly prints.

Do it up in plaids, but cut your squares on the bias if you do!

For bias-cut squares, you will need approximately one-and-a-half times as much fabric. A 12 ½-inch square cut on the bias is 17¾ inches across. (See the chart in "Raggedy Edges" on page 30 for fabric requirements.)

Choose contrasting colors for the inner and outer areas. Choose fabrics with small, consistent patterns for the inner areas. Large, busy prints will be lost.

Fabric requirements

(Yardages are given for squares cut on the straight of grain; variations in yardages for bias-cut squares are shown where necessary.)

Inside	1½ yards green; for bias cutting, add ½-yard
Outside	2 yards burgundy; for bias cutting, add ½-yard
Border	½-yard (included in burgundy)
Batting	⅔-yard of 45 inches wide

Cutting plan

Green	Nine 12½-inch squares
	Four 2-inch strips for border
Burgundy	Nine 12½-inch squares
	Four 3-inch strips for border
	Two 2½- by 4½-inch end blocks
Batting	Nine 8-inch squares
	Four 2½- by 27-inch strips for border

Layout

Three across and three down.

Specific instructions

1. Refer to the "Basic Square" instructions, beginning on page 23.
2. Prepare nine square units and join in three rows of three units each.
3. The project is shown with a pieced border. Pieced strips are used in place of the solid strips shown in the "Border" instructions in Chapter One, page 14. To make a solid border for this project, substitute four 4½-inch strips for the pieced strips.

"Country Petals" uses the principles of the basic square. Shown here is a 28-inch square made by Laura Farson and quilted by Cindy Marshall.

4. Sew one 2-inch strip of green to one 3-inch strip of burgundy. Repeat with the remaining border strips.

5. Two sides of the project have border strips with the inner part green and the outer part burgundy. The other two sides have the green and burgundy strips with end blocks that form the corner squares when folded.

6. To prepare the strips with end blocks, cut two of the green/burgundy strips to ½-inch plus the length of the unfinished side.

7. Sew a 2½- by 4½-inch burgundy block across each end of these two cut strips. (Refer to illustration 1.19 in the "Borders with Corner Blocks" section of Chapter One, page 15.)

8. With the inner fabric along the raw edge of the project, sew the first two striped strips to the project's two opposite sides. Continue following the instructions in the "Border" section, page 14.

9. Insert a 1½-inch strip of batting between the folded border layers. Trim it to fit between the seam allowances.

10. With the inner fabric along the raw edge of the project, sew the pieced strips with burgundy corners to the remaining opposite sides of the quilt, matching the corners.

11. Fold back and topstitch as instructed in "Turning Back Petals," page 20.

Batik Watercolor
Basic Square

Finished size: 28 inches square
Difficulty level: Easy
Block size: 8-inch square

The beauty of Batik fabric is in its unpredictability. This is very evident in the petal area of this quilt.

Choose fabrics that are fairly consistent for the inner areas. Busier prints will be lost. Higher contrast between the inner and outer fabrics will highlight the petal shapes more.

This is also a perfect quilt to make any size. Just sew the desired number of blocks, sew into strips, and join.

Fabric requirements

Inside	Nine fat quarters mixed watermark Batiks (large enough for bias cutting)
Outside	1½-yard Batik coordinate; add ½-yard for bias cutting
Border	½-yard Batik, inner strip
Border	¼-yard of one of the inner fabrics, outer strip
Batting	⅔-yard of 45 inches wide

Cutting plan

Mixed fat quarter	One 12½-inch square of each fat quarter, preferably cut on the bias
	Four 3¾-inch-wide strips for border of one inner fabric
Batik	Nine 12½-inch squares, preferably cut on the bias
	Four 1½-inch-wide strips for border
Batting	Nine 8-inch squares

Layout

Three across and three down

Specific instructions

Prepare nine square units and join in three rows of three units each.

A basic square design does not have to be basic at all when you throw Batik fabric into the mix. Shown here is a finished "Batik Watercolor" 28-inch square made by Laura Farson and quilted by Cindy Marshall.

Border instructions

1. Sew one 1½-inch strip of Batik fabric to one 3¾-inch border strip.
2. Repeat with the remaining border strips. These pieced strips are used instead of a solid piece of border fabric.

In this project, corner blocks are not inserted, so the outside "binding" area is broken at the corners. If this does not appeal to you, substitute four 4¾-inch solid strips for the pieced border strips.

3. Sew the uncut strips to the first two opposite sides of the border by following the "Border" instructions in Chapter One, page 14.
4. Sew the remaining strips to the unfinished sides of the quilt.
5. Fold back and topstitch petals as instructed on page 20, "Turning Back Petals."

Raggedy Edges
Basic Square

Finished size: Four blocks makes a 16½-inch square. Six blocks by eight blocks (48) measures 50 by 66 inches.
Difficulty level: Easiest
Block size: 8¼-inch square

Make this one in every color! A 6- by 8-block group makes a great lap robe. Cozy flannels are as snuggly as one gets. Homespun means country! Make it manly with plaids. Or, try it in pastels for grandma and primaries for babies and school kids.

Fabric requirements for every five blocks

Note: In the "Bias" section of on page 12, there is a cutting diagram for 12½-inch blocks (See 1.5). For each yard of fabric, five 12½-inch blocks can be cut.

Inside	1 yard cream flannel or neutral homespun
Outside	1 yard plaid flannel or homespun
Binding	1¾-inch-wide strips multiplied by the number needed (See "Binding," page 12.)
Batting	(optional) ¼-yard for five blocks of 45-inch-wide batting

Cutting plan

Cream	Four 12½-inch squares, cut on the bias
Plaid	Four 12½-inch squares, cut on the bias
Batting	Four 8-inch squares

Specific instructions

See the "Raggedy Edge" section on page 25 of Chapter Two. The most important point is to cut the blocks on the bias. If you don't, you'll have spaghetti when you wash it!

1. Join the longest rows first.
2. Fold back the joined petal areas in the middle.
3. Sew the rows together in pairs.
4. Bind, wash, and dry.

Other sizes using common sizes of rulers

Block cut size	Batting cut size	Finished square	Fabric/No. of blocks
12½ inches	8 inches	8¼ inches	1 yard/5 squares
9½ inches	6 inches	6¼ inches	1 yard/10 squares
15 inches	9¾ inches	10 inches	2 yards/8 squares
6 inches	3½ inches	3¾ inches	1 yard/72 squares

Warm and fuzzy flannels are great made into "Raggedy Edges," shown here as a 16½-inch square made by Laura Farson, 2000.

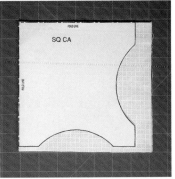

2.6 Place the template along the fold edges of the square, making sure there is no fabric showing on the straight edge of the template.

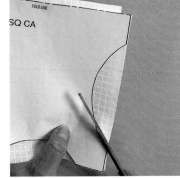

2.7 With scissors, cut through four layers along the raw edges of the template.

2.8 After cutting is complete, open the folded piece, and press it flat.

Helpful Hint

♦♦♦

A walking foot or dual-feed is useful for step 3 under "Construction."

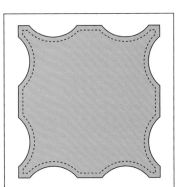

2.9 Follow the cutaway edges and curves of the outside fabric piece to sew a 1/4-inch seam. Reduce stitch length at points.

Cutaway Squares

For an elegant, clean look, choose the cutaway square. The fold-back area of the petal is eliminated, leaving an open, gentle arc of layered fabric.

This design lends itself to table linens as it has clean, sleek lines. Choose fabrics with larger prints for the outside and smaller prints or tone on tone for the inside. Because the design is so distinct, large busy prints detract from it.

Since larger petal areas are revealed, batting is desirable.

A finished block will measure $8\frac{1}{2}$ inches square.

Template

Copy template CASQ12 (page 114) once and cut it out along the solid line.

Cutting plan

1. Cut $12\frac{1}{2}$-inch squares of front fabric on the straight of grain.
2. Fold the square in half and then in half again to form a square with two folded sides. Press carefully so that the raw edges are very even.
3. Spray the backside of the template with temporary adhesive spray.
4. Place the solid sides of the template along the fold edges of the fabric square, checking to be sure that there is no fabric showing along the straight edge of the template. (See 2.6)
5. Cut through four layers along the cutaway sides (raw edges) of the template with scissors. Keep the layers of fabric even while cutting. Pinching the area near the scissors helps. If you have a circle-shaped plastic template matching the curve, cut on a mat with a rotary cutter along the curve. (See 2.7)
6. Once cut, open the folded piece. (See 2.8)
7. Press flat.
8. Cut the inside fabric into $12\frac{1}{2}$-inch or larger squares.

Construction

1. Place a cutaway outside piece right-side down on an inside square, matching the straight edges.
2. Pin the corners and center areas along the sides.
3. Sew $\frac{1}{4}$-inch seam, following along the cutaway edges and curves of the outside fabric piece. Reduce the stitch length at the points. (See 2.9 and Helpful Hint)
4. Trim the seam allowance evenly with scissors to approximately $\frac{1}{8}$-inch. Be careful not to get too close to the stitching. Snip across the outside corners.
5. Press flat.
6. With the inner fabric facing up, cut a slash 2 inches long through **just one layer**, across the bias at a point that will be hidden by a folded corner flap. Avoid cutting across the area that will fall into the fold. (See page 24 for a Helpful Hint to assist with this step.)

Fast-Folded Flowers

2.10 Be sure the batting is centered, and the edges are even.

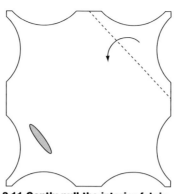

2.11 Gently pull the interior fabric through the slash to turn right-side out. Watch the corners and points.

2.12 Get fancy with your topstitching! Showcase those special stitches, or try an unique thread.

Batting

Batting is necessary in this style because of the larger exposed petal areas.

1. Fuse an 8-inch square of batting on the diagonal to the wrong side of the outside fabric.
2. Place the piece of batting so that it is centered, and edges are even. (See 2.10)
3. Turn the piece right-side out by gently pulling the interior fabric through the slash. Pay special attention to the corners and points so that all the fabric is turned to the seam allowance. (See 2.11)
4. Press the cutaway square flat, making sure the seam allowances are fully open.
5. Fold the corners to the center forming a square. Align the points in the center so that the corners lie flat and even. Press.
6. Prepare the remaining cutaway squares in the same manner.
7. Arrange the units as shown in the project or in your own pattern.

Joining

1. Once the arrangement is finished, join the units together. Joining the rows in the longest direction makes managing sections easier.
2. Open the touching flaps of two units. Match the fold lines and pin. (See 1.22 in "Joining," page 16)
3. Sew in the fold.
4. Replace the flaps and repeat for units along the row.
5. Once rows are joined, pin two rows together and sew in the folds for the length of the row.
6. Join rows into pairs, and then join the pairs into sections.
7. Once all the sections are joined, add binding, if desired.

Binding

1. Measure the four sides of the project. To this number add 24 inches for the corner turning. Divide this total by 40 inches, the length of a typical selvedge-to-selvedge strip.
2. Join the strips and bind as instructed in the "Binding" section of Chapter One, page 12.
3. Topstitch the outlines of the cutaway petals. This is the perfect place to show off special stitches and fancy threads! (See 2.12)
4. Press.

Floral Shadows
Cutaway Square

Finished size: 25 inches square
Difficulty level: Easy
Block size: 10 inches square and 5 inches square

Show off your fancy stitches by outlining the petal areas of this project. The smooth, arced edges give this a very tailored look. Use combinations of small and large squares to make table linens.

Fabric requirements

Inside	1½ yards cream
Outside	1½ yards blue
Binding	(optional) ⅓-yard blue
Batting	½-yard of 45 inches wide

Templates

CASQ15	Large cutaway square (page 117)
CASQ7	Small cutaway square (page 115)

Cutting plan

Cream	Four 15-inch squares
	Nine 7¾-inch squares
Blue	Four 15-inch squares folded twice and cut with template CASQ15
	Nine 7¾-inch squares folded twice and cut with template CASQ7
Binding	(optional) Four 1¾-inch-wide strips
Batting	Four 10-inch squares
	Nine 4¾-inch squares

Specific instructions

Follow the instructions in the "Cutaway Squares" section of Chapter Two, page 32. Prepare four large and nine small units.

Layout

See the project photograph on the next page.

Joining plan

1. Join four pairs of two small blocks.
2. Divide the joining into three rows. The first row includes one large block, two small blocks set vertically, and one large block. The second row includes five small blocks joined in a horizontal row. And the third row is the same as the first.
3. Join row one to row two and the bottom of row two to row three, matching the corners.
4. Bind, if desired.

This design may be called "Floral Shadows," but you'll certainly not want to hide it in the shadows! The cutaway square technique is optimal for showing off fancy stitching skills. This 25-inch square was made by Laura Farson, 2001.

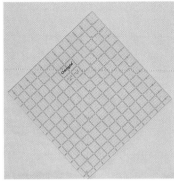

$Helpful$ $Hint$

◆◆◆

This and other techniques are designed to utilize standard-sized square rotary rulers.

2.13 Cut a square of outside/background fabric

2.14 Press open with the seam allowance toward the center square.

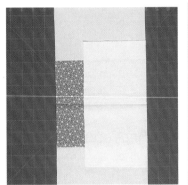

2.15 Center the rectangles on the remaining two sides of the square.

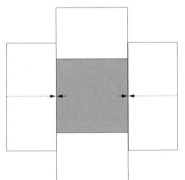

2.16 Sew and press the seam allowances toward the accent square. Trim bulky corners.

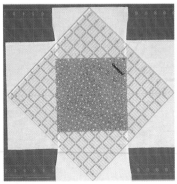

2.17 Place a square ruler on the diagonal. Place the outermost ¼-inch lines of the rotary ruler on the intersections between the accent fabric and the center square.

Accented-Petal Squares

This is a wonderful enhancement to the square. A petal outline fabric accents these pretty squares.

The color, when sufficiently contrasting to the background and inside, will show off the petal effect by forming an outlined area. Use colors that either contrast sharply or are otherwise well defined.

The petal-accent area, formed by turning back the inside of the triangle pieces, looks most attractive in a solid or tone-on-tone fabric.

The inside of the petals lends itself to small prints, as larger ones may not show consistent color throughout. One of the colors taken from the inside and outside print would produce a unifying look.

The outside fabric is the background for the petal area and the backside of the quilt; as such, it dominates the look of the project. Since this fabric is not manipulated like the petals, it lends itself to busier and/or larger prints. It can be either a coordinate or total contrast to the interior fabric.

Cutting plan

1. Cut one 8-inch square of inside petal fabric
2. From one 5½-inch strip of accent fabric, crosscut two 5½- by 8-inch rectangles and two 5½- by 11-inch rectangles.
3. Cut one 12½-inch bias square of outside/background fabric. (See 2.13) Also, refer to the "Bias" section of Chapter One, page 12, for a cutting diagram (illustration 1.5).

Construction

1. Place two 5½- by 8-inch accent rectangles right-side down on two opposite sides of an inside fabric square, matching the seam lines.
2. Sew ¼-inch seams along both sides.
3. Press open with the seam allowance toward the center square. (See 2.14)
4. Fold the square in half with one accent piece on top of the other.
5. Press crease lines in the center and edges of the square by lightly touching the iron to the center and both edges.
6. Using the crease lines to center them, place the 5½- by 11-inch rectangles centered on the remaining two sides of the square. (See 2.15)
7. Sew and press the seam allowances toward the accent square. Trim bulky corners. (See 2.16)
8. Place a 12½-inch square ruler on the diagonal. Place the outermost ¼-inch lines on the rotary ruler on the four intersections between the accent fabric and the center square. Visually verify the accurate placement of the ruler by checking to see that all the extra fabric around the edges is the same size. (See 2.17)
9. Trim excess fabric, using the ruler and rotary cutter. (See 2.18)

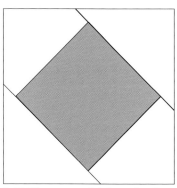

2.18 Trim excess fabric, using the ruler and rotary cutter.

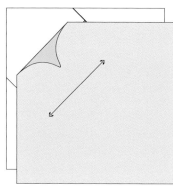

2.19 Match the raw edges and pin.

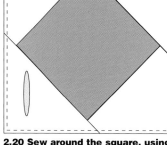

2.20 Sew around the square, using a dual-feed or walking foot and crossing the stitching at the corners.

10. With right sides together, place this 12½-inch outside square of fabric onto the right side of the trimmed square piece.
11. Match the raw edges and pin. (See 2.19)
12. Sew around the square, using a dual-feed or walking foot and crossing the stitching at the corners. (See 2.20)
13. Trim the seam to approximately ⅛-inch using a ruler and rotary cutter.
14. With the accent fabric facing up, cut a 3-inch-long slash through just one layer across the bias in one of the corners about 1 inch from the corner.

Note: Since the corner fabric is a bias-cut edge, your slash will be parallel to the side of the square.

Batting

The very lightest and thinnest works best. (Try Goldfuse, Quilt Light, or Thermore.)

1. If batting is desired, cut 8-inch squares of batting.
2. Spray-fuse or press-fuse to the inside of the backside fabric.
3. Turn the piece right-side out by gently pulling the fabric through the slash. Pay special attention to the corners so that all the fabric is turned to the seam allowance.
4. Press the square flat, making sure the seam allowances are fully open.
5. Fold the corners to the middle of the inside square so that the sides of the flaps lie flat and even. (See 2.21)
6. Press.
7. Prepare the remaining squares in the same fashion.
8. Once the squares are complete, arrange them as shown in the project or in your own pattern.

Joining

1. Once you have the arrangement complete, sew the units together.
2. First join across rows, and then join these groups in pairs of rows. This method keeps the sections manageable in the sewing machine.
3. Open the flaps of two touching squares.
4. Match the seam/fold lines, and pin across them.
5. Sew in the fold. (See 2.22)
6. Replace the flaps to their unit. It may be helpful to pin the flaps to keep them out of the way.
7. Repeat for all the squares in a row.
8. Join two rows at a time.
9. Join the pairs of rows together, using the joints as guides to match accurately.

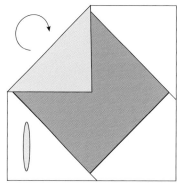

2.21 Fold the corners to the middle of the inside square so the sides of the flaps lie flat and even.

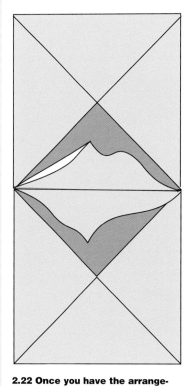

2.22 Once you have the arrangement complete, open the folds and sew the units together.

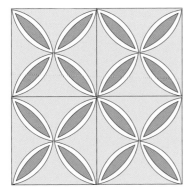

2.23 Completed accented-petal squares should look like this.

Binding

Bind the outside edges of the project with a single layer of fabric.

1. Cut a number of fabric strips 1¾ inches wide to equal the total distance around the project's borders plus 24 inches for the corners.
2. Refer to the "Binding" section in Chapter One, page 12.

Forming petals

1. Begin at the center or a corner of a square. Place three to four stitches in the flap before turning the edge back to reveal the inner fabric, and sew along this edge.
2. As you approach the center or outside corner, return the flap to its original unturned position and topstitch for three to four stitches. This forms a flat center and flat outside corner.
3. Repeat this process without stopping by crossing over the corners and centers to turn back all the flaps. (See 2.23)
4. Press.

Granny's Yellow
Accented-Petal Square

Finished size: 50 by 67 inches
Difficulty level: Intermediate
Block size: 8⅜-inch square

If you love the reproduction fabrics, this is a great quilt to show off your stash! It's where mine is.

There are so many ways you can make this quilt. Change the outside color to match your décor. Mix and match using plaid shirting and make the petal areas plain. Petal-accents will glow when made of gold. Or for a dramatic effect, use black petal outlines and jewel color petals for a "stained-glass" look.

Fabric requirements

Inside	Twenty-four fat eighths
Outside	9 yards yellow in one length
Petal-accent	7⅓ yards white muslin
Binding	½-yard (included in yellow)
Batting	2 yards of 45 inches wide

Cutting plan

Fat eighths	Two 8-inch squares of each of twenty-four fabrics
Yellow	Forty-eight 12½-inch squares cut on the bias
	Seven 1¾-inch strips for binding
White	Forty-eight 5½-inch strips, and then crosscut each of them into two 5½- by 8-inch rectangles and two 5½- by 11-inch rectangles
Batting	Forty-eight 7¼-inch squares

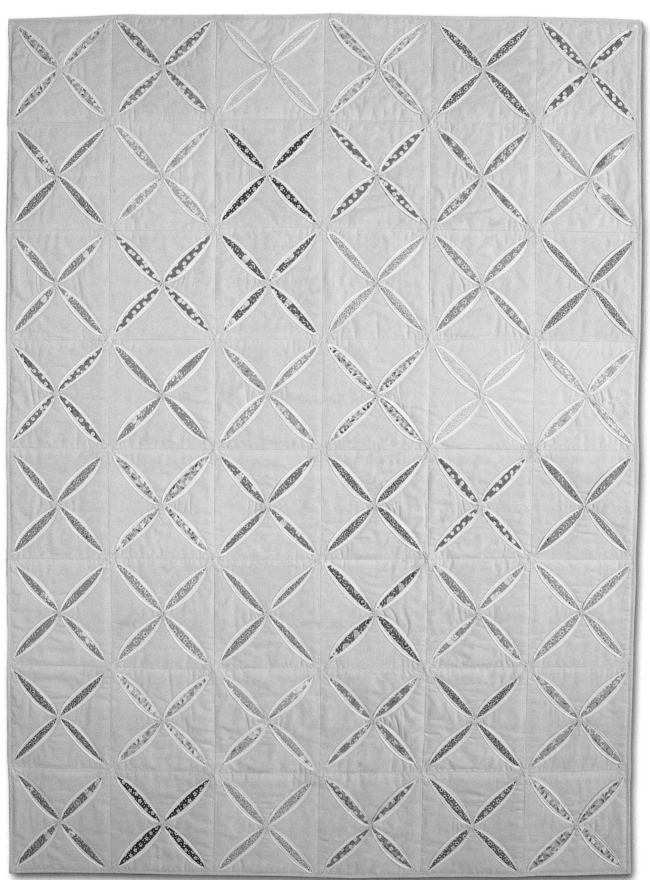

When you think of a typical "grandmotherly" quilt, "Granny's Yellow" probably isn't what you had in mind. Versitility is the key to this exciting design, shown here at 50 by 67 inches; made by Laura Farson, 2001.

Helpful Hint

♦ ♦ ♦

Chain-piecing saves time
when doing a large
number of units.

Specific instructions

1. Follow the instructions in the "Accented-Petal Squares" section of Chapter Two, page 36.
2. When cutting the forty-eight bias squares from one 9-yard piece, you will need to cut five squares from every yard. (Refer to the "Bias" section of Chapter One, page 12, for the cutting diagram plus the squares that fall "between" the five, illustration 1.5.)
3. Fold the fabric selvedge to selvedge.
4. Place a 12½-inch square ruler on point at the folded edge.
5. Cut through both layers (i.e. two squares at once).
6. Move the ruler so that its point meets the previous cut-point. There will be a triangle on the fold between the cut areas. This is a folded 12½-inch square.
7. Unfold and trim to size.
8. Repeat until you have forty-eight squares.

Layout

Six rows of eight blocks.

1. Arrange the blocks to scramble the colors as much as possible. Balance light and dark shades, but don't overplan. Be spontaneous! (Refer to the "Joining" and "Binding" sections of Chapter One, pages 16 and 12.)

2.24 Variety will really enhance the "Petals and Ribbons" design. It is the most unique of the square-based units.

Joining

1. Join eight blocks to make rows.
2. Join two rows.
3. Fold back the center-joined petal areas and topstitch. These long strips are easier to manage in the sewing machine at this point. Be careful not to sew down areas that need to be joined.
4. Join the paired rows, fold back the petals, and topstitch.
5. Bind with the seven joined 1¾-inch yellow strips.

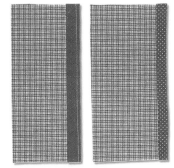

2.25 Place an accent strip right-side down on an outside rectangle, and sew along the long edge.

Petals and Ribbons Squares

"Petals and Ribbons" is the most unique of the square-based designs. It has a little more going on during construction, but it's worth the extra effort.

Because there are four elements to the front side, there is a myriad of possibilities.

The "Petals and Ribbons" design works well with variety in the outside fabric, as well as in the accents. Fat quarters are perfect for mixing and matching these components. For a more geometric look, limiting to two sharply contrasting bold colors – such as navy and yellow – can work well. (See 2.24)

Cutting plan for each square

Four 11- by 5-inch rectangles of outside fabric
Four 11- by 1-inch strips of accent fabric
One 12½-inch square of backing fabric, which will outline the front of each piece
One 12½-inch square of inside fabric

Construction

1. Place an accent strip right-side down on an outside rectangle, matching the long edges.
2. Sew along the long edge. (See 2.25)
3. Repeat for the other three rectangles and accent pieces. (See Helpful Hint)
4. Fold the pieces, right sides together, so that the accent strips are folded in half.

"Petals and Ribbons" designs will take extra effort to put together, but your diligence will be rewarded with the myriad of possibilities this design allows.

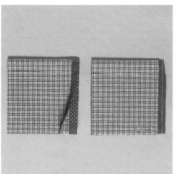

2.26 From the raw edge of the fold, sew along the accent strip.

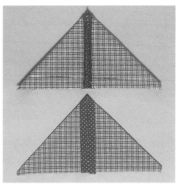

2.27 Flip to the right side and open to form a triangle.

2.28 Use the 45-degree line on the ruler to trim the bottom edge of the triangle accurately.

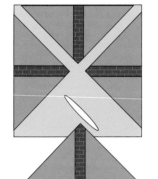

2.29 Match the center of the triangles to the center points onto outside edges of the square.

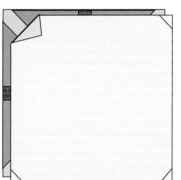

2.30 Place an outside fabric square right-side down on top of the pinned triangles.

2.31 Trim to 1/8-inch along the seam allowance and across the corners to reduce bulk.

Petals and Ribbons Squares construction continued

5. Sew along the raw edge of the accent strip from the raw edge to the fold. (See 2.26)
6. Chain-piece the three others.
7. Trim the point at the fold and finger-press the seam open.
8. Fold the rectangle in half and finger-press the center. Use this fold to center the front seam of the triangle.
9. Flip to the right side and open to form a triangle. (See 2.27)
10. Trim the bottom edge of the triangle with a rotary cutter and ruler so that both edges are even and the triangle measures 5¼ inches from base to point. Use the 45-degree line on the ruler, as illustrated in the picture. (See 2.28)
11. Assemble the pieces on a rotary mat so that you can cut the slash after step 15.
12. Fold the inside fabric square in half, and finger-press the center points along the sides.
13. Repeat in the other direction.
14. Place the four triangles right-side up along the outer edges on the right side of the inside square.
15. Match the center of the triangles to the center points pressed onto outside edges of the square. There will be gaps at the corners of the inside square. (See 2.29)

Cutting the slash

1. Lift one triangle and make a 2-inch slash with a rotary cutter across the bias in the center of the area covered by the triangle piece.
2. Pin the corners of the triangles to the square so that the pinheads are hanging over the outside edge of the square.
3. The corners of this block are not square. This "cut-off" corner is sewn using a guideline. To create this guideline, make a template by folding a 1¼-inch paper square in half diagonally.
4. Place the triangle template over the corner on the wrong side of the fabric.
5. Draw a line with a fabric marker along the angled edge.
6. Place an outside fabric square right-side down on top of the pinned triangles. (See 2.30)
7. Pin at the corners away from the seam line.
8. Sew along the raw edges and ¼-inch inside the drawn lines, crossing the stitching twice at each of the diagonal corners.
9. Trim to approximately ⅛-inch along the seam allowance and across the corners to reduce bulk.(See 2.31)

Fast-Folded Flowers

2.32 Turn the piece right-side out by gently pulling the fabric and triangles through the slash.

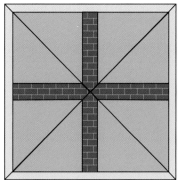

2.33 Fold the triangles to the center. Be sure to match the accent stripes and edge areas.

2.34 Repeat the process with the needle at the corner, folding over the petal and topstitching.

Batting

If batting is desired, the lightest/thinnest works best, as this design has lots of layers and seams.

1. Cut 10¾-inch squares of batting.
2. Spray-fuse or press to the wrong side of the outer fabric.
3. Turn the piece right-side out by gently pulling the fabric and triangles through the slash. (If you forgot to make the slash, make one now.) Pay special attention to the corner areas so that all the fabric is turned to the seam allowance, and the triangle flaps are flat. (See 2.32)
4. Press flat.
5. Fold the triangles to the center; match the accent stripes and edge areas. (See 2.33)
6. Repeat for the number of units in the project.
7. Arrange the units according to the project instructions or your plan.

Joining

1. Join units along the longer row first.
2. Open flaps that touch, match the accent stripes (which are between the layers being sewn together), and pin across the fold line.
3. Sew in the fold. (It is very helpful to use a walking foot at this point.)
4. Repeat for all the blocks in a row and then for all the rows. (See Helpful Hint)
5. Return the flaps to the center of their blocks and press.
6. Pin at the center of the accent stripes.
7. Topstitch along both edges of the accent stripes and across the points at the center of the units.

Binding

Bind the outside edges of the project with a single layer of fabric. (Refer to the "Binding" section of Chapter One, page 12.)

Turning back the petals

1. On the front side of the project, set the sewing machine needle into the corner where the triangle meets the edge of the project.
2. With the presser foot lifted, fold back the edge of the triangle.
3. Lower the presser foot and sew along the edge of the petal formed by this turned-back fabric. The flap will be narrower at the corners and wide in the center. The best look will be achieved when the fold is not forced, but gently eased for a consistent distance.
4. When one petal is complete, sew to the next corner.
5. Repeat the process with the needle at the corner, folding over the petal and topstitching. (See 2.34)
6. Press the project.

Helpful Hint

♦♦♦

When joining, it is easier to manage the sections in the sewing machine if you join two rows at a time and then join the two pairs. Join the rows together by opening the adjacent flaps, matching the joints and stripes (again, check between the layers being sewn together), and sewing in the fold close to the seam line.

Peachy Petals
Petals & Ribbons Square

Finished size: 22 inches square
Difficulty level: Intermediate
Block size: 11 inches square

Peachy describes just how yummy this project is. Because of the linear nature of this block, plaids and wavy stripe fabrics work wonderfully. Create warm masculine tones with flannels and homespun fabrics. Limit your colors for a very tailored look.

Fabric requirements

Inside	⅔-yard cream print
Front	1 yard peach plaid
Back	⅔-yard peach print
Accents	¼-yard peach dot
Batting	⅓-yard of 45 inches wide

Cutting plan

Cream	Four 11-inch squares
Print	Four 11-inch squares
Plaid	Cut three 11-inch strips and crosscut into sixteen 5½- by 11-inch rectangles
Peach dot	Cut six 1-inch strips and crosscut into sixteen 1- by 11-inch strips
Batting	Four 10-inch squares

Specific instructions

1. Follow the instructions in the "Petals and Ribbons" section of Chapter Two, beginning on page 40.
2. This block doesn't require binding. Secure the corners when joining by backstitching or using the "tie-off" feature of your sewing machine.

You will feel just peachy wrapped up in this "Peachy Petals" design. The example above was made by Laura Farson, 2000.

Hugs and Kisses
Petals & Ribbons Square

Finished size: 42 by 63½ inches
Difficulty level: Intermediate
Block size: Twenty-four
10½-inch squares

This project has a very tidy and elegant look. These colors have a fresh, light, springtime feeling, but you could make it in reds and greens for the winter holidays. Feel free to add ribbons and bows, and give it as a "prewrapped" gift!

Fabric requirements

Green	2 yards
Blue	2 yards
Yellow	2 yards
Pink	2 yards
Purple	1½ yards
Inside	3 yards antique white
Batting	2 yards of 45 inches wide

Cutting plan

Cut from each of the first four colors:

	Twenty 5½- by 11-inch rectangles for fronts
	Twenty 1- by 11-inch strips for accents
	Five 12½-inch squares for backs
Purple	Sixteen 5½- by 11-inch rectangles for fronts
	Sixteen 1- by 11-inch strips for accents
	Four 12½-inch squares for backs
Antique white	Twenty four 12½-inch squares
Batting	Twenty-four 10-inch squares

Specific instructions

The instructions for this pattern have been updated to improve joining. As a result, there will be an outline of fabric surrounding the blocks as shown in the "Peachy Petals" photograph on page 45 and in the other examples on pages 40 (See 2.24) and 41.

The design of this pattern matches the back fabric square to the front fabric, which decreases the visibility of this outline. If you want to accentuate the outline, as in the other examples, scramble the backside pieces or choose a contrasting color fabric such as white or black.

Follow the instructions in the "Petals and Ribbons" section of this Chapter, beginning on page 40. There are five units of the first four colors and four units of purple. From each of the fabrics, cut front squares, accent strips, and a back square in the quantities shown in the cutting plan. Scramble the accent strips among the blocks.

"Hugs and Kisses" is likely what you'll receive from anyone getting this design as a gift. This example was made by Laura Farson, 2000.

Layout

Four rows of six blocks.

1. Join six blocks into a row and join rows in pairs.
2. Secure the edges by backstitching or using the "tie-off" feature of your sewing machine.

3 triangles

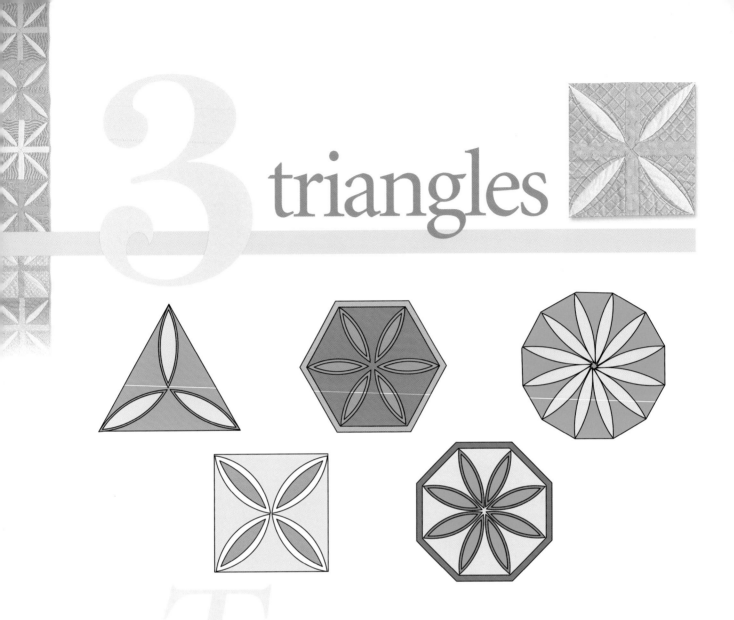

*T*riangles provide more colors in smaller spaces, are easy to handle, and are easy to join in rows. With color variation and shading, they can look like tumbling blocks with flower petals.

Triangles are handy to use as filler pieces between hexagon units. When made with three petal flaps, they can be used to join groups of units. Triangle units create exciting variety.

This chapter will describe how to make basic triangles with two parts. It is possible to make triangles with cutaway or shadow petals, but the process is a bit tricky.

Choose two colors: one for the inside and one for the outside; one color for the outside and a variety for the inside; or mix and match colors for the inside and the outside. The "Golden Petals" centerpiece project uses only two fabrics.

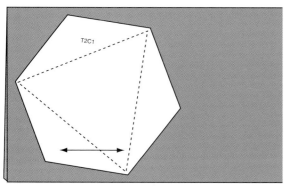

3.1 Place the hexagon-shaped template T2C1 on the folded fabric, being careful to orient the grain line marking.

Helpful Hint

◆◆◆

Place the front and back fabrics right sides together before cutting the hexagon shapes. These pairs are ready to sew.

Basic Two-Piece Triangles

By their nature, six equilateral triangles make a hexagon. The advantage of using triangles instead of hexagons is that you can include a greater number of colors in the background and/or in the petals. The outside piece forms the back of the unit and the area around the petal. The inside fabric forms the petal-reveal and the petal-outline areas.

In this chapter, you will learn how to make the equilateral triangle with three flaps. Two fabrics are cut into hexagon shapes. An outside fabric hexagon is sewn to an inside fabric hexagon. The unit is trimmed, batting applied, and a small slash cut before turning it right-side out and pressing. Sewing in the fold inside the flaps joins the units.

Equilateral Triangle Instructions

Once you have decided which fabric(s) will be outside and inside (those for the petals), fold the individual pieces selvedge to selvedge, and then fold again, matching the fold to the selvedge and creating four layers.

Template preparation

1. Make two photocopies of template T2C1 (page 118) and cut along the outer solid lines.
2. Tape the two halves together to make a hexagon-shaped template.

Cutting plan

1. Place the hexagon-shaped template T2C1 on the folded fabric, being careful to orient the template using the "grain line" marking. Edges are bias-cut to facilitate turning back the petals. (See 3.1)
2. Place a rotary ruler, with the ¼-inch line on top of the dotted line of the template.
3. Cut along the edge through all four layers, using the ruler and rotary cutter. You will have four pieces. Repeat this until you have the total number needed for your project.
4. Repeat this procedure with the petal fabric.

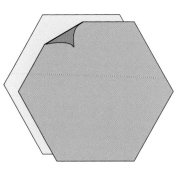

3.2 Place one hexagon-shaped piece of outside fabric on one of inside fabric, matching the straight edges and points.

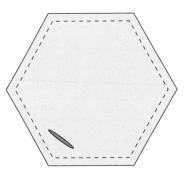

3.3 Sew along all sides, crossing the stitching at the corners. With the inner fabric facing up, cut a slash through one layer.

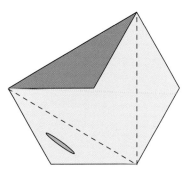

3.4 Press the hexagon flat, making sure the seam allowances are fully open.

Helpful Hint

◆◆◆

It's easy to trim using the ruler and rotary cutter.

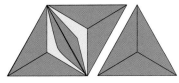

3.5 Open the flaps of two touching triangles.

Construction

1. Then, with the right sides together, place one hexagon-shaped piece of outside fabric on one of inside fabric, matching the straight edges and points. (See 3.2)
2. Pin at the corners to secure the bias edges.
3. Sew along all sides, crossing the stitching at the corners. (See 3.3)
4. Trim the seam allowance back to approximately ⅛-inch, being very careful not to get too close to the stitching. (Refer to the photo in the "Trimming" section of Chapter One, page 19.)
5. Snip across the corners to smooth them.
6. With the inner fabric facing up, cut a slash 2 inches long through just one layer, across the bias in one of the corners about 1½ inches in from the point. (See 3.3)

Batting

1. If batting is desired, prepare a batting template.
2. Make two photocopies of the hexagon-shaped template H3C1 and tape them together.
3. Cut it out along lines drawn between alternate corners that form a triangle. Use this triangle-shaped template to cut the batting.
4. Spray-fuse or press-fuse a triangle of batting to the wrong side of the outside fabric.
5. Turn the piece right-side out by gently pulling the fabric through the slash. Pay special attention to the corners so that all the fabric is turned to the seam allowance.
6. Press the hexagon flat, making sure the seam allowances are fully open.
7. Fold three alternate corners to meet in the center to form the triangle. Align the edges so that the corners lie flat. (See 3.4)
8. Press.
9. Prepare the remaining hexagons in the same manner. If you have many fabrics, separate them into two groups designated as background or petals.
10. Once the triangles are complete, arrange them as shown in the project or in your own pattern. Note that similar colors will blend together, and the pattern will be lost. More contrast will show the separate triangle shapes. (See 3.6)

Note that some of the petals are folded back into angular shapes rather than curves. This is another option.

Joining

1. Once you have the arrangement complete, sew the units together. Sewing the triangle units in rows makes joining simple.

3.6 Petals can be folded at angles as well as curves.

2. Once a row is joined, a second row can be sewn to it. Even with just six triangles, as in the centerpiece project, joining two groups of three units simplifies the process.
3. Open the flaps of two touching triangles. (See 3.5)
4. Match the fold lines of the flaps with right sides together. Pin across the fold.
5. Sew along the fold line. Fold back the flaps to their respective units.
6. Press again to set the seams, and pin the flaps at the center.
7. If desired, attach a binding as explained in the "Binding" section of Chapter One, page 12.
8. Turn back the petals and topstitch by machine or a hand-sewn method. (See 3.7)
9. Refer to the "Turning Back Petals" section of Chapter One, page 20, to complete the project.

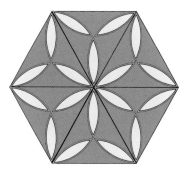

3.7 Turn back the petals and topstitch by machine or a hand-sewn method.

Golden Petals Centerpiece
Two-Color Triangle

Finished size: 17 by 19½ inches
Difficulty level: Easy
Block size: 8½ inches high by 9¾ inches wide

This basic project is simple to make but lovely to look at. Six triangles join to make a hexagon centerpiece. Place a flower arrangement on it to complete the scene.

Fabric requirements

Inside	⅔-yard gold
Outside	⅔-yard green
Batting (optional)	⅓-yard of 45 inches wide

Templates

T2C1 (page 116)	One copy
H3C1 (page 121)	Two copies

Cutting plan

Gold	Six hexagons
Green	Six hexagons
Batting	Six 7½- by 9-inch triangles

Specific instructions

1. Follow the directions for the "Basic Two-Piece Triangle" in this chapter, beginning on page 49.
2. Batting, although optional, would be better protection for a table. If desired, spray-fuse or press a triangle of batting to the inside of the back fabric before flipping the unit right-side out.
3. A triangle template can be cut for the batting. On your H3C1 hexagon template, draw a line between every other corner of the stitching line.
4. Cut out this triangle template and use it for the batting template.
5. Join two rows of three triangles and then join the two rows in the center. This project is unbound; therefore, the joined areas should be secured by back-stitching.
6. Press.

It can't get any better than the "Golden Petals" project: simple to make, yet lovely to look at. The above example was made by Laura Farson, 2000.

4 hexagons

he nifty thing about hexagons is that they look flowery, and they can nest together so there are fewer filler pieces to make.

The basic hexagon is made up of two six-pointed, star-shaped pieces of fabric. One color is for the inside and one for the outside.

There are two ways to make this unit. One is to cut both the inside and the outside fabric into star shapes. These cutout stars are placed right sides together and sewn along the edges. These edges are all on the bias.

As an alternative, you can cut out just the inside pieces into star shapes and then match them to outside fabric squares. The inside fabric star is placed on the bias of the outside fabric, but since only one piece has cut-bias edges, the sewing is easier. This way requires more fabric, but I recommend it for your first project.

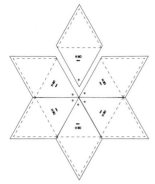

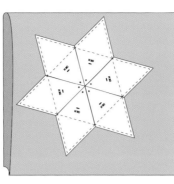

4.1 Matching the centers, tape the six diamonds together to form a star-shaped template.

4.2 Place the template on the fabric with no edges parallel to the grain line.

Basic Hexagon

Preparing the template

1. Photocopy template H2C on page 120 six times.
2. Cut along the solid lines on all six copies.
3. Matching the centers, tape the six diamonds together to form a star-shaped template. Three sections make a straight line. Use the lines on the rotary mat to line up each half of the template. (See 4.1)

Cutting plan

1. Organize your fabric choices into one pile for the inside and one for the outside.
2. Cut the outside fabric into enough 20-inch squares for the number of outside pieces needed.
3. After deciding which fabrics to use, fold the inside fabric selvedge to selvedge. This assumes that you will be cutting out two star shapes at a time. If only making one star piece of a color, use only a single layer of fabric.
4. Spray the backside of the paper template with temporary adhesive spray (See the "Adhesive" section in Chapter One, page 11.)
5. Place the template on the fabric with no edges parallel to the grain line. All edges are cut in a bias direction. (See 4.2)
6. Place a rotary ruler, with the ¼-inch line on top of the dotted line of the template and the end of the ruler stopped at the end of the template.
7. Cut through both layers of fabric along the edge of the ruler with a rotary cutter. Avoid cutting through the seam allowance at the inside corners. (Olfa's rotary-point cutter is handy to cut the inside corners.)
8. Move the ruler around the template and repeat the cutting until the entire star is cut. There are two layers and thus two stars.
9. Repeat this procedure for all the inside fabric(s) until you have the number of pieces required for your project.

Construction

1. Place one inside fabric star and one outside fabric square right sides together.
2. Rotate the star-shaped piece so that it does not have any edges going with the grain line of the outside fabric.
3. Pin in the points to secure the bias edges.
4. Sew along all sides, crossing the stitching at the points. (See 4.3)
5. Trim the seam allowance to approximately ⅛-inch from the stitching, being very careful not to get too close. (See Helpful Hint at right.)
6. Snip across the outside corners to smooth them and clip inside corners to ease the turning. This work is easily done while waiting for an appointment. Keep a roll of tape or lint roller handy to collect the debris!

Helpful Hint

◆◆◆

Use a walking foot to keep the edges flat. If you have a tie-down feature on your sewing machine, it is helpful to use it at both the inside and outside corners. Otherwise, decrease stitch length at these corners.

4.3 Sew along all sides, crossing the stitching at the points.

Helpful Hint

◆◆◆

I've done the trimming (step 5 of "Construction) with a rotary cutter and ruler, but invariably, I slip across the stitching at some point. Therefore, I recommend using a scissors.

4.4 Cut a slash 2 inches wide through just one layer, across the bias in the central area of the hexagon.

Basic Hexagons continued

At this point, check again to be sure which fabric is for the outside and which is for the inside.

Making the slash

1. With the inside fabric facing up, cut a slash 2 inches wide through just one layer, across the bias in the central area of the hexagon. (See 4.4)
2. Before cutting, check to be sure that it falls under a folded flap.
3. To make the slash, lift a single layer of fabric at about the center of its intended location.
4. Pinch it into a tiny fold and snip across the fold. (Again, be sure you only have one layer of fabric!)
5. Then, insert your scissors into the snip and cut first 1 inch in one direction and then 1 inch in the opposite. Cutting along the bias keeps the slash from fraying.

Batting

Use of batting is optional, but in many cases, it is desirable. It's very easy to include because it's added as a small piece within each unit. (Refer to the "Batting" section in Chapter One, page 12.)

1. The simplest way to cut batting is to make a template. Photocopy the H3C1 hexagon-shaped template on page 121 twice. Cut out the two halves on the dotted lines, and tape the halves together.
2. With the batting out of the package, carefully unfold it.
3. Refold into four layers.
4. Cut a strip of batting the same width as the batting template.
5. Place the batting template on the strip.
6. Place a rotary ruler on the template and line up the edge of the ruler with the edge of the template. Cut through four layers of batting.
7. Repeat until you have the number of batting pieces needed.

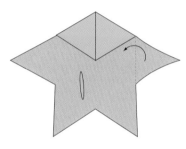

4.5 Align the points so that the corners lay flat.

Attaching the batting

1. Align the piece of batting on the wrong side of the outside fabric, so that it is centered.
2. Leave a ¼-inch space around the edge. This is the area that will be joined.
3. Fuse the batting to the fabric by pressing or by spraying it with temporary adhesive.
4. Turn the piece right-side out by gently pulling the fabric through the slash. Pay special attention to the points so that all the fabric is turned to the seam allowance. And be sure the batting is flat. If not, go inside the slash with your finger and smooth it out.
5. Press the star shape flat, making sure the seam allowances are fully open. (A mini-iron works well for this step.)
6. Fold the points to the center, forming a hexagon.
7. Align the points so that the corners lay flat. (See 4.5)
8. Press.
9. Prepare the remaining hexagon stars in the same manner.
10. Once the hexagons are complete, prepare the edge-filler triangles and corners.

Edge-Filler Triangles

Construction

1. Photocopy template HST on page 119 and cut along the solid lines.
2. For each edge-filler piece, cut two HST pieces: one from inside fabric and one from the outside fabric.
3. Place an inside and an outside piece with the right sides together. (See 4.6)

4.6 Place an inside and an outside piece with the right sides together. Sew along the seam line.

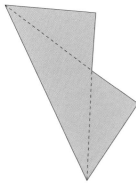

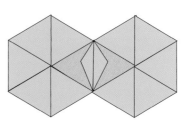

4.7 Turn right-sides out and press, making sure that the seam allowance is fully open.

4.8 Fold the upper points along the lines shown in the illustration to form a triangle.

4.9 Open the folded points of two adjacent units. Match the fold, and sew in the fold.

4. Sew along the seam line, which is the angled area indicated along the top of the unit in the illustration. (See 4.6)

5. Trim along the seam allowance and clip the inside corner.

Batting

1. If you are using batting, prepare a batting template.

2. Make a photocopy of HST and cut it out on the inside of the triangle-shaped dotted line.

3. From the cutoffs of the hexagon-shaped batting pieces, cut enough triangle-shaped batting for the edge-filler triangles.

4. Keep the batting piece(s) about ¼-inch from the stitching line, as this is the area that will be sewn through when joined.

5. Spray-fuse or iron the batting onto the wrong side of the outside fabric of the filler triangle.

6. Turn right-sides out and press, making sure that the seam allowance is fully open. (See 4.7)

7. Fold the upper points along the lines shown in the illustration to form a triangle. (See 4.8)

Joining

1. Arrange the units as shown in the project or in your own pattern.

2. Once the arrangement is complete, sew the units together. (It is easier to join the horizontal seams first, creating vertical sets.)

3. Open the folded points of two adjacent units. Match the fold, and sew in the fold. (See 4.9)

4. Press.

5. Once all the horizontal seams are sewn together (See "A" in illustration 4.10), add the edge-filler triangles. (See "B" in 4.10)

6. Fold back and topstitch the flaps flat on the edge triangles.

7. Turn back and topstitch the center petal flaps on the vertical strips. (See "C" in illustration 4.10)

8. Join the vertical strips. You will zigzag back and forth between the hexagons.

9. Finish by folding back and topstitching the remaining petal areas. (See "D" in illustration 4.10)

10. Bind the outside edges with a single layer of fabric. Refer to the "Binding section of Chapter One, page 12.

As an alternative arrangement, make extra hexagon units and cut them horizontally or vertically as needed. (See 4.11)

4.10 Joining is made simple when you concentrate on one vertical grouping at a time.

4.11 There are numerous variations to the hexagon design, including this flowery project made from a circle of seven hexagons surrounded by four horizontal and six vertical halves. Five additional hexagons were cut to fit the edges, and a two-color binding was made without corner blocks.

Fall Festival
Basic Hexagon

Finished size: 47 by 50½ inches
Difficulty level: Intermediate
Block size: 11 inches wide by 9⅞ inches high

Put the accent on "Fest." Ole! It's a whirlwind of color – big and bright!

Make it in primary colors for the kids. This is the best example of mix-and-match colors.

Or, for a more subdued look, use just one color outside and mix up the petal colors.

Fabric requirements

Color	Yardage	Inside stars	Outside 20-inch squares	Total	Edge-fillers inside/outside
Gold	3½	7	5	12	3/3
Rust	3	4	6	10	0/2
Green	3	4	6	10	3/1
Multiprint	3	6	4	10	3/3
Brown	2½	4	4	8	1/1
Binding	½	Multiprint	Eight 2-inch strips		
Batting (45 inches)	2½				

Templates

H2C	Hexagon	Six copies
HST	Side triangle	One copy
H3C1	Batting	Two copies taped together

Cutting plan

1. Following the chart above, cut twenty-five inside stars from the fabrics listed using the hexagon star template H2C, page 120.
2. Cut twenty-five 20-inch squares in the colors and quantities indicated.
3. Cut eight 2-inch-wide strips of the multicolor print for the binding.
4. Cut twenty-five batting pieces using a hexagon-shaped batting template prepared from H3C1, page 121.

Specific instructions

1. Follow the directions in the "Basic Hexagon" section of Chapter Four, beginning on page 55. You will also need ten edge-filler triangles.
2. Prepare twenty-five two-color hexagons, mixing the inside and outside colors. Use the project photo on the opposite page as a guide.
3. Make ten edge-filler triangles with mixed colors.

Looking to make a statement with big and bright colors? This "Fall Festival" design, shown above 47 by 50 inches, is your answer.

Layout

1. Arrange the hexagon units, half-hexagons, and edge-filler pieces according to the project photo.
2. Join vertical rows of hexagons first.
3. Turn back and topstitch the center petal flaps before joining the rows in pairs. As you join each pair of rows, turn back and topstitch the petal areas.
4. After all rows are joined, bind the quilt.

If you like color-placement options, try the "Accented-Petal Hexagon" like the 32-by 45-inch example above made by Laura Farson and quilted by Cindy Marshall.

Accented-Petal Hexagons

The "Accented-Petal Hexagon" pattern has more options for color placement than a basic hexagon design. The third color of fabric can be positioned to outline the edge of the petal area or focus attention on the petal background area surrounding the petals. Switching the inside and outside of the unit's construction shifts the position of the third fabric. By mixing and matching color options, diverse effects are possible.

The project "Petals in the Ferns" is an accented-petal hexagon, Version One. The petal-reveal areas are outlined with contrasting fabrics. The outside piece that forms the backside and the petal-surround is a folded hexagon star. The backside pieces and fillers are all green to serve as a background for the flower shapes.

Selective petal turning and subtle differences in the petal-accent fabric make this window and "broken glass" effect, as in the "French Petals" design pictured on the opposite page.

For a leaded glass look, use black for the petal-accent triangles and bright colors for the petal-reveal of the inner hexagon piece.

The accented-petal unit is a hexagonal, star-shaped piece.

In Version One, the inside of the star is a hexagon with six triangles sewn to it. These triangles form the outline of the flower petal when turned back. The hexagon fabric shows as the center of the petals. The outside of the star is a single piece of fabric that, when folded, forms the back of the unit and the front side of the triangles.

In Version Two, the pieced hexagon and triangle are on the outside of the unit. The front-facing triangles can be fussy-cut to create a fancy pattern. The hexagon

Helpful Hint

◆◆◆

Try white muslin. I often make petal outlines using white muslin for the triangle pieces because it has such a high contrast, and white goes with almost everything!

"French Petals" uses an accented-petal hexagon design to create a window effect. The above quilt is 40 inches square; made by Laura Farson, 1999.

part forms the back of the unit and folds over the outer edge of the front to form an outline. The inner fabric is a single, whole, hexagon-shaped star. It shows as the petal-reveal and the petal turn-back areas.

The construction of the two versions differs only in the placement of the turning slash. To keep the slash hidden within the folds of the unit, the slash is cut in the hexagon piece for Version One. For Version Two, the slash is cut in the star piece that forms the inner portion of that unit. The instructions for both versions are included in this section of the chapter.

Preparing the templates

1. Photocopy template H3C1 on page 121 twice and H3CT on page 122 once.
2. Cut the two half-hexagons and the triangle shapes along the outside solid lines.
3. Tape the two halves of the hexagon together along the centerline.
4. With a pointed object, such as the tip of a stiletto or the point of a compass, poke a hole at each of the six corners of the dotted line of the hexagon template. These points form the intersection of the fold line and the seam allowance. They will be used to mark the corners of the seam line on the fabric hexagons.

Fabric preparation

1. Choose three fabrics (one for the hexagon, one for the triangles, and one for the outside). When choosing your fabrics, keep in mind that there will be many triangle-shaped pieces left from cutting out the hexagons. (See 4.12 on the next page) These can be used with other hexagons in the same project, or

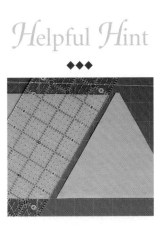

4.12 Place the hexagon-shaped template H3C1 on the folded fabric designated for the hexagon. Because triangles form when the hexagon is cut, you will want to save these end scraps for later use.

Helpful Hint

♦♦♦

Spray a little temporary adhesive on the back of the template to keep it from slipping while cutting.

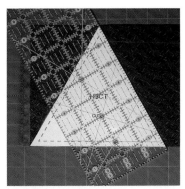

4.13 Place a rotary ruler on top of the template, with the ¼-inch line on top of the dotted template line.

Helpful Hint

♦♦♦

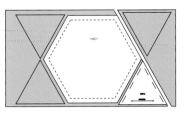

In step 15, you may notice that the 60-degree line of the ruler will line up with the edge of the fabric. If you are familiar with the use of this line, the triangles may be cut by alternating the 60-degree line of the ruler along the long edge of the fabric strip.

plan to use them in another project teamed up with other fabric hexagons.

2. Fold the outside fabric selvedge to selvedge.
3. Cut two 18½-inch squares through both layers, along the selvedge edge. Cutting the squares along the selvedge leaves a nice long piece along the folded side.
4. Fold the hexagon and triangle fabrics, selvedge to selvedge and fold to selvedge, creating four layers.
5. Place the hexagon-shaped template H3C1 on the folded fabric designated for the hexagon, being careful to orient the template with the grain line. Note that there is a natural triangle formed when the hexagon is cut. These triangles can be used with other color hexagons to make the petal turn-back area. (See 4.12)
6. Place a rotary ruler on top of the template with the ½-inch line on top of the dotted line of the template.
7. Using the ruler as the rotary cutter guide, cut along its edge.
8. Cut around all six sides, through all four layers. You will have four pieces.
9. Repeat this until you have the total number needed for your project.
10. Place the H3C1 hexagon-shaped template on the backside of a fabric hexagon.
11. With a fabric-marking pencil, mark the points where the seam allowance meets the fold line, using the holes you poked into the template. Repeat this marking for all the hexagons.
12. Cut the triangle fabric into 5-inch selvedge-to-selvedge strips.
13. With the grain line along the cut edge of the fabric, place template H3CT on the fabric strip.
14. Place a rotary ruler on top of the template with the ¼-inch line on top of the dotted line of the template. (See 4.13)
15. Using the ruler as the rotary cutter guide, cut along its edge.
16. Repeat until you have six triangles for every hexagon piece.
17. After cutting the four layers, unfold the 5-inch strip and cut the remaining fabric into two triangles.

Fussy-cut triangles

One of the reasons to use a Version One unit is that you can fussy-cut your triangles. By cutting the six triangles from the same part of the fabric design, you can create a whirled or kaleidoscope appearance.

1. Make a plastic triangle template by tracing template H3CT onto template plastic with a permanent marker.
2. Pick a place on the fabric that looks interesting. Cut it out using the plastic triangle template.
3. Trace a part of the fabric design onto the plastic with the marker.
4. Use this marked triangle to cut five more triangles that are exact replicas of

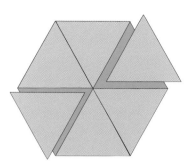

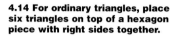

4.14 For ordinary triangles, place six triangles on top of a hexagon piece with right sides together.

4.15 Join the triangles to the hexagon by sewing 1/4-inch from the edge around all six sides.

4.16 Rotate the star-shaped piece so that all edges are cut on the bias. Pin at the points.

the first one.

5. In the next step, place the fabric triangles right-side up on the hexagon, so that the "top" of each is in the center of the hexagon. Preview other patterns formed by the duplicated triangles, by rotating the part of the pattern that is placed in the center of the hexagon. Choose the arrangement that pleases you, and flip the triangles over to match right sides together. Skip to step 2 in the next section.

Construction

1. For ordinary triangles (not fussy-cut), place six triangles on top of a hexagon piece with the right sides together and the grain line of the triangles along the cut edge of the hexagon. (See 4.14)

2. Join the triangles to the hexagon by sewing ¼-inch from the edge around all six sides, crossing the stitching lines at the corners. It's helpful to use a dual-feed or walking foot. (See 4.15)

3. Trim the seam to approximately ⅛-inch along the sides of the hexagon.

4. Press the triangles open with the seam allowance toward the triangles. This forms a six-pointed star.

5. Place this star-shaped piece onto the square of star fabric, right sides together.

6. Rotate the star-shaped piece so that all edges are cut on the bias. (See 4.16)

7. Pin at the points to secure the bias edges.

8. Sew along all the edges of the pieced star, making the inner corner turns at the dots marked on the hexagon.

9. Decrease the stitch length as you approach the corner dot and for a ½-inch after making the turn. This is an inside corner that will be stressed during the turning process. (See Helpful Hint)

10. Cross the stitching lines at the points. These areas will be trimmed quite close, and the shorter stitches will keep them from pulling out when turned.

11. Using scissors, cut out the star-shaped piece ⅛-inch from the seam line, being careful not to get too close to the stitching.

12. Trim the outside points and clip the inside corners to ease the turning.

Batting

Use of batting is optional, but in many cases, it is desirable. It's very easy to include because it's added as a small piece within each unit.

1. For ease, use a template. Photocopy the H3C1 template (hexagon-shaped) made previously, and cut it out inside the dotted line.

2. Unfold the batting as it comes out of the package.

3. Refold it into four smoothed layers.

4. Cut a strip of batting the same width as the batting template.

5. Place the batting template on the strip.

6. Place a rotary ruler on the template and line up the edge of the ruler with the

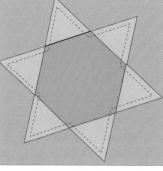

Helpful Hint

◆◆◆

In step 9, it's a good idea to shorten your machine's stitch length around the outside of the points and at the inside of the corners. These areas will be trimmed quite close, and the shorter stitches will keep them from pulling out

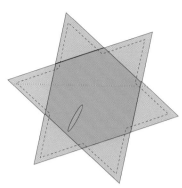

4.17 For Version One, cut a slash 2 inches wide through just one layer, across the bias in the hexagon-shaped piece.

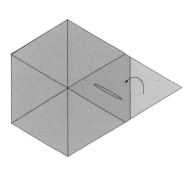

4.18 Fold the six points to the center so that the flaps lie flat and the points meet without gaps. Version One will look like this.

4.19 For Version Two, face the star-shaped piece up and cut the slash through just one layer.

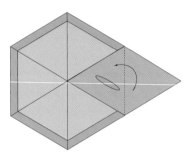

4.20 A Version Two unit will look like this when the flaps are folded flat.

edge of the template.

7. Cut through four layers of batting.

8. Repeat until you have the number of batting pieces needed. (Save the cutoffs for use later in filler pieces.)

Attaching the batting

1. Align the piece of batting on the wrong side of the fabric so that it is centered between the inner corners of the backside star.

2. Leave a little space all around the edge.

3. Spray-fuse or press-fuse the batting to the fabric.

Cutting the slash (Version One)

For Version One, the slash is cut on the bias in the hexagon-shaped center piece of fabric.

1. Before cutting, fold a point over the area to be sure a folded petal will cover the slash.

2. With the inner fabric facing up, cut a slash 2 inches wide through just one layer, across the bias in the hexagon-shaped piece about 1½ inches in from where the fold will be. (See 4.17)

3. Turn the piece right-side out by gently pulling the fabric through the slash. Pay special attention to the corners so that all the fabric is turned to the seam allowance. (See "Turning Right-Side Out," page 20.)

4. Carefully finger-press the seam open before pressing with an iron to make the process easier. Press the star shape flat.

5. Fold the six points to the center so that the flaps lie flat and the points meet without gaps. (See 4.18)

6. Press.

Cutting the slash (Version Two)

For Version Two, the slash is cut in the center area of the star-shaped inner piece.

1. Before cutting the slash, fold a point over the area to be sure that the folded flap will cover the slash.

2. With the star-shaped piece facing up, cut the slash through just one layer. Refer to the "Slash" section of Chapter Once, page 18. (See 4.19)

Turn right-side out, and press as instructed in steps 3 through 6 in the Version One slash-cutting instructions. A Version Two unit will look like illustration 4.20.

4.21 Place two rectangle halves right sides together and stitch across the short side, leaving a 1½-inch opening.

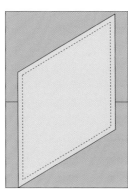

4.22 Place the front-fabric diamond on the rectangle, right sides together.

Filler Pieces

Hexagons can be arranged two ways. Units can be nestled together as in the "Fall Festival" project shown in the "Basic Hexagon" section, page 58. Or, they can be set point-to-point as in the "Petals in the Ferns" project at the end of this section, page 68.

Instructions for the side filler pieces and half-hexagons used in the nestled version are included in the Basic Hexagon section.

In this section, instructions are given for diamond-shaped filler pieces.

Diamond Filler Pieces

Pillow-style filler pieces are advantageous over the awkward joining of multi-sided, flapped pieces. Diamond filler pieces have no flaps. Rather, they are like little pillows with double layers of batting inside to match the thickness of the adjacent hexagonal units.

Diamond filler pieces are used whole between four hexagons set point to point.

Cut in half horizontally, they fill in at the top and bottom edges.

Along the side, diamonds are cut vertically. These filler pieces are set on the backside of the project overlapping the space between units.

On the front side, the hexagon-flaps are opened and the pieces are joined through the overlapped area under the flaps.

Construction

1. Photocopy template H3CD on page 123 and cut it out on the outer solid line.
2. Cut front fabric into diamonds, using the template, ruler, and rotary cutter.
3. Cut the back fabric into 6- by 11-inch rectangles and cut these in half, leaving 5½- by 6-inch rectangles.
4. Place two rectangle halves right sides together and stitch across the short side, leaving a 1½-inch opening. This opening will be used later to flip the diamonds right-side out. (See 4.21)
5. Press the rectangle open and flat.
6. Place the front-fabric diamond on the rectangle, right sides together. (See 4.22)
7. Sew along the outside edges, crossing the stitching at the corners.
8. Trim the seam allowance to approximately ⅛-inch.
9. Spray-fuse or press a smaller diamond-shaped piece of batting to the inside of the front fabric. There are usually enough cutoffs from the hexagon batting to fill in the center area of the diamond. Use two triangle-shaped pieces or four right triangles for this area.
10. Leave ¼-inch along the edge of the seam lines free of batting, as this area will

Helpful Hint

♦♦♦

As an alternative to nesting the hexagon blocks, diamond filler pieces are simpler to join.

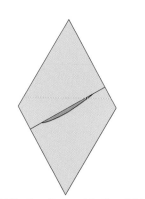

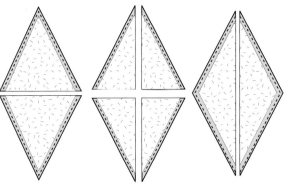

4.23 Flip the diamond to the right side by gently pulling the outer fabric through the opening left in the back fabric.

4.24 Cut the sewn diamond horizontally or vertically, depending on the number needed for your project.

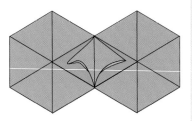

4.25 Open the petal flaps of two touching hexagons. Match the fold lines, pin together, and sew in the fold.

be sewn through during the joining process. Having batting too near the fold causes lumps.

11. Flip the diamond to the right side by gently pulling the outer fabric through the opening left in the back fabric. Pay special attention to the points and corners so that all the fabric is turned to the seam allowance. (See 4.23)

12. Press.

Diamonds that are to be cut horizontally or vertically can be made by sewing two whole diamond-shaped pieces together.

1. Cut front and back diamond-shaped pieces.

2. With right sides together, place a front diamond on a back diamond.

3. Sew around all sides.

4. Fuse a double layer of batting to the center area. Use the cutoffs from the hexagons.

5. Cut the sewn diamond horizontally or vertically, depending on the number needed for your project. (See 4.24)

6. Cutting a diamond into four pieces makes corner triangles. The finished edge will be at the corner.

7. The cut edges will be bound.

Joining

1. Arrange the pieces according to the project or your own design.

2. Once the arrangement is complete, sew the units together. (It is easier to join the horizontal seams first, creating vertical strips.)

3. Open the petal flaps of two touching hexagons. (See 4.25)

4. Match the fold lines, pin together, and sew in the fold.

5. Join all the touching hexagons into vertical strips. You may want to fold back and topstitch the center petal areas before joining. (See part "A" in illustration 4.26)

Joining the filler diamonds

1. Place two joined strips of hexagons right-side down on your work area with the points of the hexagons touching.

2. With the opening facing the back of the project, place whole diamond-filler pieces so they evenly overlap the space between the hexagons. The top and bottom points of adjacent diamonds will overlap.

3. Pin the diamonds onto the back of the hexagons, catching just one layer of hexagon fabric.

4. Alternatively, place masking or other easily removable tape at 2-inch intervals along the diamonds. For photos of this technique, refer to the "Filler Units" section in Chapter Six, pages 105 through 107.

5. Turn the grouped pieces to the front. Open the petal flaps of the hexagon

Fast-Folded Flowers

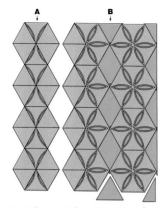

4.26 Join touching hexagons into vertical strips. Then use filler diamonds to join strips together.

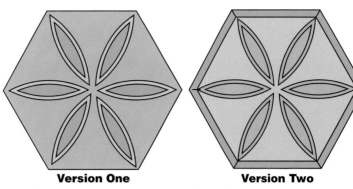

Version One   **Version Two**

4.27 Version One hexagons have contrasting outlines around the petal areas. Version Two units, with triangles on the outside, have an outline around the edge of the hexagon.

units that lie over the filler piece and pin across the fold of the flaps.

6. Sew along the fold lines and through the overlapping areas of the filler unit, being careful not to catch the petal flaps in the seam.

7. Return the flaps to their original folded position and pin to the center of the hexagon.

8. Repeat for each of the filler diamonds. Some adjustment to the upper and lower overlapping points may be necessary.

9. Once you have joined two vertical strips of hexagons, you may want to fold back and topstitch the petal flaps in those hexagons that are already joined. (See "B" in illustration 4.26)

10. Press.

Border/Binding

1. Refer to the "Border" and "Binding" sections of Chapter One for instructions, pages 14 and 12.

2. Prepare and apply border or binding fabric strips per the project instructions.

3. Complete the petal flap turning and topstitching.

The Version One hexagons have contrasting outlines around the petal areas.

Version Two units, with triangles on the outside, have an outline around the edge of the hexagon. (See 4.27)

Helpful Hint

◆◆◆

In larger projects, the joined fabric pieces become quite large and unwieldy. By doing some of the topstitching as you go, you can avoid some of the wrestling with the larger pieces later.

Petals in the Ferns
Accented-Petal Hexagon
(Version One)

Finished size: 34 by 38 inches
Difficulty level: Intermediate
Block size: 8⅜ by 9¾ inches

This quilt evokes memories of a spring hike through dense woods. It's shear delight to find a cluster of bright blossoms poking through the damp leaves.

Choosing a mix of shades creates light and dark areas. For overall consistency in appearance, limit the petal areas to just two colors.

Fabric requirements

Inside	⅔-yard each of four shades of pink, or 2⅔- yard of one fabric
Outside	3⅓ yards green for squares
	¾-yard green for backside of diamonds
Border	½-yard fern/leaf green for border
Diamonds	¾-yard fern/leaf green
Batting	2 yards of 45 inches wide

Templates

H3C1	Hexagon	Two copies taped together
H3CT	Triangle	One copy
H3CD	Diamond	One copy

Cutting plan

Green (tone on tone)		Twelve 18½-inch squares
		Twelve 6- by 11-inch rectangles for diamonds
Pink	H3C1	Three hexagons each of four shades of pink
Pink	H3CT	Twenty-four triangles from each of four shades of pink
Fern	H3CD	Twelve 6- by 11-inch diamonds
		Four 4½-inch-wide border strips
Batting		Twelve hexagons cut on the inside line of template H3C1
		Four 1¾- by 38-inch strips for border
		Save cutoffs for filling diamond pieces

Specific instructions

1. Follow the instructions in the "Accented-Petal Hexagon" section of this chapter, beginning on page 60.
2. Make twelve pink and green hexagon units and twelve diamond-shaped filler pieces.
3. Make six whole diamonds with openings.
4. Cut the other six diamonds as follows: two horizontally, one into fourths for the corners, and three vertically for the sides.
5. Arrange the pieces as shown in the project photo.

"Petals in the Ferns," shown above 34 by 38 inches, expresses the delight experienced by finding a cluster of bright blossoms poking through fern leaves on the floor of the forest.

6. Join the units in three columns of four units each. You may wish to fold back the petals and topstitch the center areas of each strip before joining them. This makes it easier to manage in the sewing machine at this stage.

7. Sew the four border strips as instructed in the "Border" section of Chapter One, page 14.

Helpful Hint

♦♦♦

Be sure to read through
the special instructions
for four-color hexagons
before starting your
project.

Four-Part Hexagons

The "Four-Part Hexagon" pattern gives you the greatest flexibility for color choice and placement. Because each part of the flower is a different color, really exciting effects are possible.

You can choose to make subtle shades for the outlines, or stark contrast for bright and dramatic looks.

You can use just two triangle colors and two hexagon colors for allover consistency.

It's the ultimate for a leaded glass effect, as every area is outlined.

You also may mix up the inside hexagon colors to vary the flower effects; and, as with all the other techniques, you may choose to mix and match all parts. This may turn out to be scrappy or raucous!

In the "Turkish Bazaar" project, at the end of this chapter, note how the dark petal edges stand out against the red background, and the outer edge is defined by the second red print.

The technique for making these units is very similar to the "Accented-Petal Hexagon." In this case, two-pieced stars are sewn together. There is an inside-pieced star and an outside-pieced star. Both are made by sewing six triangles to a center hexagon.

The inside triangles are the turn-back part of the flower petal. The inside hexagon will show as the center of the petals.

The hexagon part of the outside-pieced star shows as the backside of the project and the outline at the edge of the hexagon. The triangles sewn to it are folded toward the front and form the background for the flower.

Special instructions for four colors

Follow the instructions for "Accented-Petal Hexagons" in the previous setion of this chapter, page 60, with the following modifications. (Read through them thoroughly before beginning your project.)

1. Choose four fabrics. The inner hexagon is the petal-reveal. The inner triangle fabric forms the petal-accent. The front triangle fabric surrounds the petals, and the backside fabric outlines the outer edge of the front.

2. Using hexagon-shaped template H3C1 on page 121 and triangle template H3CT on page 122, cut each fabric into the shape designated for its position in the unit. For each unit, you will need one inner and one outer hexagon, and six each of the inner and outer triangles.

3. Mark dots through the holes in the template at the corners on the wrong side of the inner hexagon.

4. Sort your inner and outer hexagons and triangles into groups. If you are using several fabrics in more than one position, label which fabric goes where.

5. Skip the step that prepares outer squares.

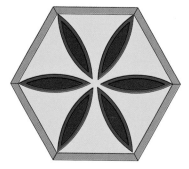

4.28 With right sides together, place an inside star on an outside star.

4.29 These two illustrations show the same unit, but with different hexagon colors in the slash. One has the red for the inner petal color and the other has orange. Note how the areas switch places when reversed.

Construction

1. Prepare an inner star-shaped unit. Following the instructions in the "Accented-Petal" section (page 60), construct an inner star from the inner hexagon and six inner triangles.
2. Press the seam allowance in toward the hexagon.
3. Prepare an outer star-shaped unit. Place six outer triangles around an outer hexagon piece with the right sides together and the grain line of the triangles along the cut edges of the hexagon. (See 4.14)
4. After trimming the triangles, press the seam allowance out toward the triangles. This is opposite from the inner piece star. In the next step, these seams will lie flat against one another.
5. With right sides together, place an inside star on an outside star. (See 4.28)
6. Match the triangles at the points and at the seam allowances that were pressed in opposite directions. Pin at the points to secure the bias edges.
7. Sew along all the outside edges of the pieced-star, making the inner corner turns at the dots marked on the hexagon and crossing the stitching at the points.
8. Trim around the sides of the joined star-shaped pieces to approximately ⅛-inch, being careful not to get too close to the stitching.
9. Trim the outside points and clip the inside corners to ease the turning.

Batting

1. With a batting template cut from a copy of H3C1, cut a piece of batting.
2. Attach the batting to the wrong side of the outer hexagon fabric with temporary adhesive or by pressing.
3. Cut the slash in the inner hexagon at a point that will be covered by a folded petal flap.
4. Continue with the turning, pressing, and folding of the hexagon unit.
5. Prepare filler units as needed by following the instructions in either or both of the "Filler Piece" sections of the "Basic Hexagon" and/or "Accented-Petal Hexagon" sections of this chapter, pages 56 and 65.

Assembly

1. Arrange the pieces according to the project or your own design.
2. Join the units and add a border or binding per the instructions in Chapter One, page 14 or 12.
3. Turn back and topstitch petals.

This unit has two looks, depending on which hexagon color is slashed and designated as the inner color. (See 4.29)

Helpful Hint

♦♦♦

It's a good idea to shorten your machine's stitch length around the outside of the points and at the inside of the corners. These areas will be trimmed quite close and the shorter stitches will keep them from pulling out when turned.

Turkish Bazaar Pillow
Four-Part Hexagon

Finished size: 18 inches square
Difficulty level: Intermediate
Block size: 10-inch hexagon

Brighten up a room with this high-contrast pillow! Red, yellow, and black look rich and exotic.

Change to primary colors for kids, or to pastels for a sunny porch. It's easy to make with just one hexagon block. Use tone-on-tone black for a rich-textured background.

Fabric requirements

Inside petals	½-yard large red print
Front triangles	¼-yard yellow print
Hexagon border	½-yard red and black small figure
Petal-accent	black (included in background)
Background	½-yard black
Backing	½-yard muslin (inside pillow lining)
Border	½-yard red small figure
Backside	½-yard black
Batting	18 inches square
Pillow form	16 inches square

Templates

H3C1	Hexagon	Two copies taped together
H3CT	Triangle	One copy

Cutting plan

Red print	One hexagon
Red outline	One hexagon
Yellow print	Six triangles
Red border	Two 3-inch-wide strips
Black backside	Two 12½- by 18-inch rectangles
Black background	One 13½-inch square
	Six triangles
Muslin	One 18-inch square

The high contrast in fabric colors of the "Turkish Bazaar" design add drama to your home decor. Pillow shown above is 18 inches square; made by Laura Farson, 2001.

Specific instructions

1. Follow the instructions in the "Four-Part Hexagons" section of Chapter Five, page 70, to make the center hexagon block.

2. Sew the six yellow triangles onto the small, red-figured outline fabric hexagon. The black triangles are sewn onto the inner large red print hexagon.

3. Complete the petal turn-back and topstitching steps.

Continued on next page.

Make this design with country ginghams and lace for a feminine pillow.

Turkish Bazaar Pillow project continued
Pillow front

1. Sew the 3-inch red outer border fabric to the 13½-inch black square.

2. With right sides together, place a red strip along one edge and sew.

3. Trim the extra fabric from the strip even with the edge of the square.

4. Repeat on the opposite side of the square.

5. Open the strips and press the seam allowance toward the red.

6. Sew the second strip along one of the remaining sides across both red strips.

7. Trim.

8. Repeat for the last side.

9. Open the seams.

10. Press the seam allowance toward the red.

11. Place the hexagon on the center of the black square.

12. Find the center by folding in half both directions and finger-pressing the folds along the edge of the black square.

13. Line up the petals with the finger-pressed folds.

14. Spray-baste the block onto the fabric or pin at the corners.

15. Turn the pieces over and layer the 18-inch piece of batting on top of the backside.

16. Cut out and remove the batting behind the hexagon.

17. Layer the muslin over the batting.

18. Spray-fuse or press-fuse the batting and muslin backing. If using temporary adhesive spray, just lift the batting and spritz with a little spray to keep it in place. Do the same for the muslin layer.

19. Turn the layered group to the front. Topstitch along the outer edge of the hexagon block with monofilament thread. (I use the hemstitch with a narrow width.)

20. Sew a straight stitch with the monofilament thread through all layers around the inside edge of the outer border.

Change the fabrics to match your home's color scheme. Above is a variation in yellow.

Pillow back

The backside of the pillow has a slotted opening for ease of turning now and for changing or laundering later.

1. Prepare the back piece by folding over 2 inches on the long side of one of the black rectangles.
2. Topstitch along the raw edge of the turned piece. It will measure 10½ by 18 inches.
3. Place this hemmed rectangle right-side down on the front of the layered piece with three raw edges even with the front square.
4. Place the unhemmed piece on top so that its sides are even with the opposite side of the square. It will overlap about 4½ inches.
5. Pin the raw edges.
6. Sew around the square.
7. Trim the corners and flip to the outside through the slot in the black square.
8. Insert the 16-inch pillow form into the slot and arrange the front so that it is unwrinkled.

5 octagons

*O*ctagons are so much fun because they have more petals and interesting filler pieces. In this chapter, you will learn how to make octagons with two, three, and four parts.

Like the other shapes, octagons can be made with as many color combinations as desired.

The procedure is identical to that of the hexagon; but as previously mentioned; filler pieces are of different shapes.

Eight is great! That could be you're mantra as you tackle the exciting possibilities an octagon can provide. Shown above is a quilt by Laura Farson that utilizes the "Basic Octagon" technique of two fabric colors.

Basic Octagons

The octagon or "stop sign" shape has eight sides. The middle space between connected units is a square. The edge units are right triangles or half-squares.

By having more petals than a hexagon, the shape is rounder and more flowery.

As with the basic hexagon, you may choose just two colors: one for the inside and one for the outside. Or, you can vary just the inside, while keeping the outside the same.

Finally, both the inside and outside can be different for a scrappier look.

Preparing the template

1. Photocopy template O2C on page 124 eight times.
2. Cut along the solid lines on all eight copies.

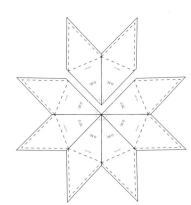

5.1 Join the halves into a star-shaped template.

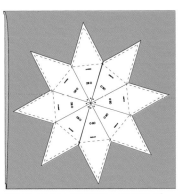

5.2 Place the template on one of the fabrics, rotated so no edge is parallel to the grain line.

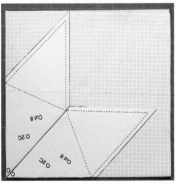

5.3 Place the template on the folded square with the center on the fabric. Line up the right-angled sides along the folded fabric edges.

3. Place two cutout copies on your rotary mat at right angles using the crossed lines of the mat as guides.

4. Matching the centers, tape the diamonds together two at a time. Four pieces form a straight line.

5. Join the halves into a star-shaped template. (See 5.1)

Fabric preparation

Organize your fabric choices into one pile for the inside pieces and one for the outside.

Outside fabric

1. After deciding which fabrics to use, fold the fabric selvedge to selvedge, and then fold again, matching the fold to the selvedge.

2. Using 45-inch-wide fabric, two 21-inch squares can be cut from each 21-inch length. Cut the outside fabric into the number of 21-inch squares needed. (I use the inch marks built into the rotary mat to make these cuts easier.)

3. Line up the fabric parallel to a horizontal line on the mat. Place the cut edge of the fabric just over the zero line.

4. Line up a ruler on the 21-inch line and cut along the edge of the ruler. This will give you a folded piece 21 inches by the width of the fabric. The easiest thing to do is just cut along the fold line. This piece will work just fine as an outside "square."

Inside fabric

From the inside fabric(s), you will cut out two stars of the same fabric at one time. If you don't want two star fabrics alike, unfold the fabric and cut through just one layer.

1. Spray the backside of the paper template with temporary adhesive spray.

2. Place the template on one of the fabrics, rotated so no edge is parallel to the grain line. All edges will be cut on the bias. (See 5.2)

3. Place a rotary ruler on top of the template, lining up the ¼-inch line with the dotted line of the template. Refer to the "Cutting" section in Chapter One, beginning on page 15.

4. Cut through both layers of fabric along the edge of the ruler with a rotary cutter. Avoid cutting through the seam allowance at the inside corners. (Olfa's rotary-point cutter is handy to cut these inside corners.)

5. Move the ruler around the template and repeat the cutting until the entire star is cut out. If you used folded fabric, there are two pieces.

6. Repeat this procedure for the number of star units needed.

Fast-Folded Flowers

5.4 Place one inside fabric star onto an outside fabric square.

5.5 Trim the seam allowance back to about 1/8-inch from the stitching, being very careful not to get too close.

Helpful Hint

◆◆◆

When sewing around the star, use your tie-down feature on your sewing machine at both the inside and outside corners; or, if not, decrease stitch length before and after crossing the corners.

Helpful Hint

◆◆◆

Trimming, as detailed in step 4 of "Construction," can be done with a rotary cutter and ruler, but there's a tendency to slip across the stitching, so I recommend using a scissors.

Alternative star-cutting procedure

This alternative is easier to cut out as four layers are cut at once, so there are fewer inside and outside corners. However, some of the edges are on the straight of grain and will be harder to turn. I suggest that you make a practice unit of each method and decide which you prefer.

1. Cut the inside fabric into 21-inch squares.
2. Fold one square in half and fold again to form a square.
3. Press the folds so that the cut edges are even.
4. Photocopy template O2C, page 124, twice.
5. Using the lines on your rotary mat, place each piece at right angles and tape together.
6. Spray some temporary adhesive on the back of the template.
7. Place this two-piece template on the folded square with the center on the folded corner. Be sure to line up the right-angled sides along the edges of the folded fabric square. (See 5.3)
8. Cut along the solid lines through all the layers.
9. Unfold, press open, and proceed.

Construction of octagon units

1. With right sides together, place one inside fabric star onto an outside fabric square, rotating the star so that all edges are on the bias. (See 5.4)
2. Pin the points of the star to secure the bias edges.
3. Sew along all the edges of the star, crossing the stitching at the points. Use a walking foot to keep the edges flat.
4. Trim the seam allowance back to approximately ⅛-inch from the stitching, being very careful not to get too close. (See 5.5 and Helpful Hint)
5. Snip across the outside corners to smooth them and clip inside corners to ease the turning.

Making the slash

1. At this point, remind yourself which fabric is for the outside and which is for the inside.
2. With the inner fabric facing up, cut a slash 2 inches wide through just one layer across the bias in the center in an area that will be covered by a folded flap.

Batting

Use of batting is optional, but in many cases is desirable. It's very easy to include because it's added as a small piece within each unit. (Refer to the "Batting" section in Chapter One, page 12.)

1. Begin by photocopying template O3C on page 125 twice.
2. Cut the two halves on the dotted line and tape them together.
3. With the batting out of the package, open and refold it so there are four layers.

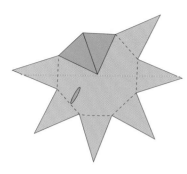

5.6 Fold the points to the center, forming an octagon as you go. Be sure to align the points so the corners lay flat.

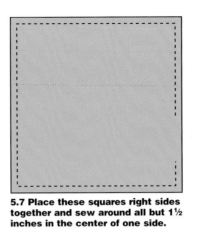

5.7 Place these squares right sides together and sew around all but 1½ inches in the center of one side.

4. Cut a strip of batting the same width as the batting template.
5. Place the batting template on the cut strip.
6. Place a rotary ruler on the template and line up the edge of the ruler with the edge of the template.
7. Cut through four layers of batting.
8. Repeat until you have the number of batting pieces needed.

Attaching the batting

1. Fuse a piece of batting to the center of the inside surface of the outside fabric.
2. Align the piece of batting so that it is centered in the octagon.
3. Leave a little space all around the edge. This is the area that will be sewn through in the joining step.
4. Turn the piece right-side out by gently pulling the fabric through the slash. Pay special attention to the points so that all the fabric is turned to the seam allowance.
5. Press the star shape flat, making sure the seam allowances are fully open. A mini-iron is useful for this step.
6. Fold the points to the center, forming an octagon. (See 5.6)
7. Align the points so that the corners lay flat.
8. Press.

Prepare the remaining octagon stars in the same manner.

Once the octagons are complete, prepare the filler squares and side- and corner-triangle units.

Filler Pieces

The spaces and edges around the octagons are filled with fabric pieces. Such pieces include:

● Pillow fillers
    a. Pillow squares – squares without flaps
    b. Edge triangle pillows – triangles without flaps
    c. Corner triangle pillows – small triangles without flaps
● Flapped fillers
    a. Squares with flaps
    b. Triangles with flaps
    c. Corner triangles

The square and triangle pillow-filler pieces are plain without flaps. The insides are filled with two layers of batting to make up for the lack of layers. These filler, or connector, pieces are overlapped on the backside of the project and sewn through the inside of the octagon flaps. (Directions follow.)

The other style of filler piece is constructed with flaps just like the octagons. The flaps of the middle squares are folded to the center and can be turned back to

The spaces and edges around the octagons are filled with flapped squares, edge triangle pillows, and corner triangle pillows. Adding a binding will finish this piece.

make smaller petal units.

Side triangles also have flaps.

When all these filler flaps are turned back, they create a very busy floral look!

Pillow Squares

On pillow squares, all edges are finished.

1. Cut two 4¾-inch squares of fabric, one each of the front and the back fabrics.

2. Place these squares right sides together and sew around all but 1½ inches in the center of one side. (See 5.7)

3. Cut and fuse together two 3¾-inch squares of batting. The batting is cut smaller so that the edge of the filler piece is not too thick. This is the area that

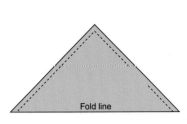

5.8 Sew along the diagonal sides, leaving a 1-inch opening along one side.

is sewn through when joining the units.

4. Spray-baste or press-fuse the batting onto the center of the square.
5. Flip to the right side through the opening in the seam allowance. Pay special attention to the corners so that they are fully open.
6. Turn the seam allowance at the opening to the inside of the square.
7. Hand- or machine-stitch to close the opening.
8. Press the square flat.

Pillow Triangles

The fabric chosen for this piece will be the same on the back as on the front. Choose a fabric that looks good on both sides of the quilt. Even if it contrasts with the backside, the pieced effect can be quite nice.

1. Cut a 4¾-inch fabric square.
2. Fold it in half diagonally with the right sides together.
3. Sew along the diagonal sides, leaving a 1-inch opening along one side. (See 5.8)
4. Cut a 3¾-inch square piece of batting, and then cut it in half diagonally.
5. Fuse these two triangles of batting to make a double-thick triangle.
6. Fuse this triangle of batting to the center of the inside of the filler triangle.
7. Flip the piece right-side out through the opening in the seam allowance. Pay special attention to the corners so that all the fabric is turned to the seam allowance.
8. Press the edges of the seam allowance so they open to the inside of the triangle.
9. Hand- or machine-stitch to close the opening.

Pillow Triangle Corners

Corner triangles are the same color on the front and backside.

1. Cut a 4¾-inch square of fabric.
2. Cut the square in half diagonally.
3. Fold each triangle in half with the right sides together.
4. Sew along the two open sides leaving a 1-inch opening. This is a half-size version of the previous example.
5. Cut a 3¾-inch square piece of batting.
6. Cut the square of batting in half diagonally, and then cut each triangle of batting in half.
7. Fuse two quarters to make a double-thick triangle. Fuse this layered batting piece to the center of the triangle.
8. Flip the triangle to the right side. Pay special attention to the corners.
9. Tuck the seam allowance at the opening to the inside and press flat.
10. Sew the opening closed with a few hand or machine stitches.

Fast-Folded Flowers

5.9 Cut two 6½-inch squares: one each of the inside and outside fabrics.

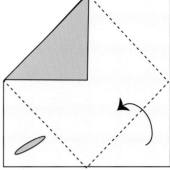

5.10 Slash in the corner across the bias and turn right-side out. Pay attention to the corners so all fabric is turned to seam allowance.

5.11 Press flat and then press the corners to the middle.

Squares with Flaps

1. Cut two 6½-inch squares: one each of the inside and outside fabrics. (See 5.9)
2. Place the two squares right sides together and stitch all the way around.
3. Spray-baste a 3¾-inch square of batting to the wrong side of the outer fabric on the diagonal.
4. Slash in the corner across the bias and turn right-side out. Pay special attention to the corners so that all the fabric is turned to the seam allowance. (See 5.10)
5. Press flat and then press the corners to the middle. (See 5.11)

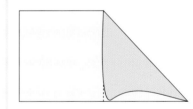

5.12 Cut the squares in half.

Corner Triangles

The corner triangle is the easiest to make. It is simply two squares of fabric folded diagonally with a triangle of batting tucked in between the layers. Because it is only used for corners, the edges can remain raw as they are incorporated into the binding.

1. Cut two 4-inch squares of fabric. One of the two must be the front fabric. The other can be the front or any inner color, as it doesn't show. Use a fabric from the project, though, so that any shadowing through will be consistent in color.
2. Place the two squares wrong sides together, matching the sides.
3. With the proper fabric on the outside, fold the squares in half on the diagonal, matching the corners.
4. Cut a 3½-inch square of batting in half on the diagonal.
5. Insert one of the batting triangles into the space between the inner and outer fabric pieces.
6. Press the fold. The cut edges will be enclosed in the border or binding.

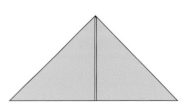

5.13 Fold the rectangle in half again with the background fabric on the outside, and gently crease the center.

Filler Triangles with Flaps

1. Follow steps 1 through 3 in the "Squares with Flaps" section above.
2. Cut the squares in half. (See 5.12)
3. Turn the rectangles right-side out.
4. Press, having fully turned the corner fabric to the outside.
5. Fold the rectangle in half again with the background fabric on the outside, and gently crease the center. (See 5.13)
6. Open.
7. Fold the seamed corners to the crease on the diagonal, forming the triangle by keeping the short-seamed sides perpendicular to the base of the triangle. (See 5.14)

5.14 Fold the seamed corners to the crease on the diagonal, forming the triangle.

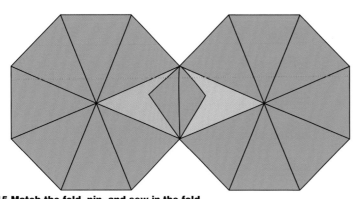

5.15 Match the fold, pin, and sew in the fold.

Helpful Hint

♦♦♦

In designing these pieces, I found that joining squares to octagons by opening the adjacent flaps of both units usually left an open hole at the corners. That's why joining the filler pieces correctly is especially important.

Organizing the pieces

1. Arrange all the pieces according to the project layout or your plan.

2. Once the arrangement is complete, sew the octagon units together. It is easier to join the horizontal seams first, creating vertical strips.

3. Open the petal flaps of two touching octagons.

4. Match the fold, pin, and sew in the fold. (See 5.15)

5. Return the petal flaps to their folded position.

Joining the filler pieces

These instructions apply to either pillow-filler pieces or flapped-filler pieces. Once all the horizontal lines of the octagon pieces are sewn together, the center squares and edge triangles are added. The filler pieces are designed to overlap the space between the octagon pieces. It is placed over the hole between the four joined octagon pieces on the backside of the project. This makes the joints fully covered.

1. Place a filler square over the space between the octagon-shaped units with the flaps of the square left folded throughout the process. Slip it through the hole to the back and line up the corners of the square with those on the octagon pieces.

2. Pin the square in position.(Refer to the photographs 6.14 through 6.16 in the "Joining" section of Chapter Six, page 107.)

3. Turn the group of pieces over and fasten the square on the back with masking tape.

4. Flip the group of pieces back to face the front.

5. Open the four petal flaps of just the octagons and pin across the fold of the flaps. I remove the tape at this point, because some tapes gum up the sewing machine needle.

6. Sew along the fold lines inside the octagon flaps and through the center square, being careful not to catch the octagon petal flaps in the seam.

7. Return the petal flaps to their original folded position and pin at their centers.

8. Repeat for each of the center square units.

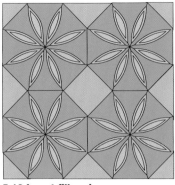

5.16 Insert filler pieces.

Attaching filler triangles

Pillow and flapped triangles can be joined just like squares.

1. Leave the flaps folded and overlap the triangle on the backside of the project.

2. Open the two octagon flaps that touch the triangle.

3. Sew through the inside of the octagon flaps. The octagon flaps are folded back to their original positions.

As an alternative, flapped triangles can be joined by sewing between the folds of the touching flaps of the triangle and the two octagons.

1. Open the flaps and match the fold lines.

2. Pin.

3. Sew through the folds. The flaps are folded back to their original positions.

This method is a little harder to do, as you have to make a turn at the peak of the triangle. Its advantage is a neater appearance when finished. (See 5.16)

4. Bind according to the "Binding" section in Chapter One, page 12.

5. Once all the pieces are joined and the binding is complete, fold back the petals on the main pieces and on the filler triangles, if desired. The flaps can be left "straight" and topstitched in place creating contrasting lines of petal fabric. Where the filler pieces are small, this is a very pleasing effect.

In the Pink
Basic Octagon

Finished size: 21½ inches square
Difficulty level: Intermediate
Block size: 8¾ inches square

Three different pinks of the same fabric group exhibit just enough shading to highlight the subtle flowery shapes. This monochromatic project has a very rich and elegant look.

Fabric requirements:

Inside	1½ yards light pink
Outside	1⅓ yards medium pink
	1 yard dark pink
Border	(included with outside fabric)
Batting	⅓-yard of 45 inches wide

Template

O2C	Octagon	Eight copies

Cutting plan

Light pink	Four octagon stars
	Three 6½-inch squares
Medium pink	Four 21-inch squares
Dark pink	Three 6½-inch squares
	Four 3½-inch squares
	Four 3½-inch strips
Batting	Four 9-inch octagons

Layout

Two rows of two.

Specific instructions

Follow the instructions in the "Basic Octagon" section of Chapter Five, page 77.

This project is made with folded filler squares. Make three whole squares. You will need one whole square and two that will be cut in half.

Making whole squares

1. Place one 6½-inch light pink square and one 6½-inch dark pink square right sides together and sew a ¼-inch seam allowance. (Refer to the instructions for flapped filler squares in Chapter Five, page 83.)
2. Make a slash; flip to the right side, press, and fold.
3. Repeat for the other two squares.

Use "In the Pink" as a throw on your little girl's bed, or add a sleeve and hang it on the wall. Either way, it brings a feminine elegance to her bedroom. The above quilt was made by Laura Farson, 2000.

Making half-squares

1. Make the four half-squares, by the same method as used for the whole squares, except cut them in half rather than making a slash.

2. Flip to the right side through the cut side, press, and fold.

3. Each corner triangle is made from two 3½-inch squares, placed right-side out and folded diagonally. These are joined with no seamed edge, as they will be encased in the border.

4. After assembling, add the 3½-inch border strips per the instructions in Chapter One, page 14.

5. Turn back and topstitch the petals.

Switching Blue
Basic Octagon

Finished size: 26½ inches square
Difficulty level: Intermediate
Block size: 8¾ inches square

This nine-block quilted wall hanging is a lesson in contrast and how it affects the appearance of a block.

Note that the center block in the example is actually made with the three-color octagon instructions. It's the same shape and size of the other eight blocks, but it looks completely different due to the reversal of dark and light.

Fabric requirements

Inside	⅝-yard light blue
	⅝-yard medium blue
	⅝-yard medium dark blue
	1¼ yards dark blue
Outside	3⅓ yards cream print
Binding	Scrap strips
Batting	¾-yard of 45 inches wide

Template

O2C	Large octagon	Eight copies

Cutting plan

Light blue	Two octagon stars
Medium blue	Two octagon stars
	Eight 3½-inch squares
Medium/dark blue	Two octagon stars
Dark blue	Three octagon stars
Cream	Nine 21-inch squares
	Sixteen 6½-inch squares
Batting	Nine 9-inch octagons

Layout

Three rows of three.

Experimenting with different contrast fabrics can dramatically affect the appearance of a block, as is evidenced in "Switching Blue," made by Laura Farson, 2000.

Specific instructions

Follow the instructions in the "Basic Octagon" section of Chapter Five, page 77.

This project is made with flapped filler squares. There is no batting in the filler squares. Make eight squares. You will need four whole squares and four that will be cut in half.

Making whole squares

1. Place two 6½-inch cream-colored squares with right sides together and sew. Refer to the instructions for "Squares with Flaps" in Chapter Five, page 83.
2. Make a slash, flip to the right side, press, and fold.
3. Repeat for the remaining three whole squares.

Continued on next page.

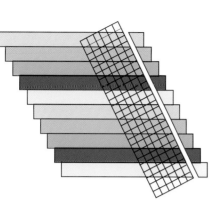

5.17 Cut ten strips from the left-over fabric scraps. Sew these strips together along the long sides with a 1-inch offset at one edge. Staggering saves fabric.

Switching Blue project continued

Making half-squares

1. To make the eight half-squares, repeat step 1 of "whole squares" (previous page). Then, cut them in half before the slash-making step.
2. Flip to the right side through the cut side, press, and fold.

Corner triangles

Each corner triangle is made from two 3½-inch squares, placed right-side out and folded diagonally. These are joined with no seamed edge, as they will be encased in the binding.

Multicolor center block

The cutting plan has an extra dark blue octagon star in lieu of the multicolor version.

1. To make a multicolor block in the center, use the "Accented-Petal Octagon" instructions on the next page.
2. Cut two triangle pieces from each of the blue fabrics. The center octagon and the inside fabric square are cream.

Special binding instructions

1. Cut ten 1¾- by at least 15-inch strips from the leftover fabric scraps. If you don't have sufficient length, join some scraps.
2. Sew these strips together along the long sides with a 1-inch offset at one edge. Staggering saves fabric. (See 5.17)
3. Press seams to one side.
4. Place a rotary ruler on the strips with the 30-degree line along the horizontal edge of the striped piece.
5. Trim off the uneven edges, and then cut eight 1½-inch strips at a 30-degree angle.
6. Sew two strips together, keeping the color sequence in order.
7. Use the four strips to bind the four sides of the project. Use the "Borders" instructions in Chapter One, page 14, to apply this binding. The striped strips are cut like border pieces rather than folded around the corners like binding.
8. Finish by turning back the petals and topstitching.
9. Press.

Accented-Petal Octagons

The "Accented-Petal Octagon" pattern can be folded two ways.

Version One

Version One forms an outline of the flower petals with a third color. This is comparable to the "Petals in the Ferns" hexagon project, page 69.

The basic unit is a star-shaped piece.

The inside of the star is an octagon with eight triangles sewn to it. These triangles form the outline of the flower petal.

The inside central octagon is the inner part of the petal that is revealed when turned back.

The triangle fabric outlines the petals.

The outside of the star is a single piece of fabric that, when folded, forms the back of the unit and the front area surrounding the petals.

Version Two

Version Two's star-shaped unit is folded the opposite way of Version One. The octagon and triangles are on the outside, and the single star-shaped fabric piece is on the inside.

The octagon-shaped piece that forms the back of the unit folds over to the front and outlines the unit.

The triangles form the front outlines of the petal area. By fussy-cutting these triangles, you can create some whirling patterns. The petal-outline and petal-reveal are the same inner fabric.

In the three Version Two projects called "Dreaming in Flowers," pages 95 through 97, notice how the front areas formed by the triangles are whirling designs. These triangles are fussy-cut. Each quilt in the series has front triangles of the same floral print. The inner fabric and the filler pieces were changed to create different effects.

Preparing the templates

1. Photocopy template O3C on page 125 twice and O3CT on page 126 once.
2. Cut the half-octagons and the triangle shapes along the outside solid lines.
3. Tape the octagon halves together to make a whole.
4. With a pointed object, such as the tip of a stiletto or the point of a compass, poke a hole at each of the eight corners of the dotted line of the octagon template. These points mark the intersection of the fold line and the seam allowance. They will be used to mark the corners of the seam line on the cut fabric octagon.

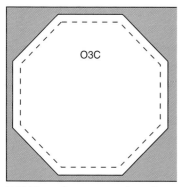

5.18 Place the octagon-shaped template O3C on the folded fabric designated for the octagon. Orient it with the grain line marking.

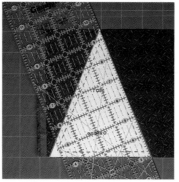

5.19 With the grain line along the cut edge of the fabric, place template O3CT on the fabric strip.

Helpful Hint

♦♦♦

Spray a little temporary adhesive on the back of the template to keep it from slipping while cutting. Place a rotary ruler on top of the template with the ¼-inch line on top of the dotted line of the template.

Construction

1. Choose three fabrics: one for the octagon, one for the triangles, and one for the star.
2. Fold the fabric chosen for the star selvedge to selvedge and then turn the fold to selvedge.
3. Cut 21-inch lengths of the folded fabric. Use the horizontal line of your rotary mat to line up the selvedge edge of the fabric. Place the cut edge just over the zero line and line up fabric along the horizontal.
4. Place a rotary ruler on the fabric at the 21-inch mark. Be sure it lines up with both the upper and lower indicator.
5. Cut along the edge of the ruler.
6. Open this 21-inch length and cut it on the first fold. The square will measure approximately 21 inches both ways, as most fabric is about 44 to 45 inches wide. Unless there is a significant shortage, this should be adequate to match with the octagon star piece.
7. Fold the octagon and triangle fabrics, selvedge to selvedge, and then turn the fold to selvedge, creating four layers.
8. Place the octagon-shaped template O3C on the folded fabric designated for the octagon, being careful to orient the template with the grain line. (See 5.18)
9. Place a rotary ruler on top of the template with the ½-inch line on top of the dotted line of the template.
10. Using the ruler as the rotary cutter guide, cut along its edge.
11. Cut around all eight sides through all four layers. You will have four pieces.
12. Repeat this until you have the total number needed for your project.
13. Place the O3C octagonal template on the backside of the fabric octagon. With a fabric marking pencil, mark the points where the seam allowance meets the fold line, using the holes you poked into the template.
14. Cut the triangle fabric into 5⅛-inch selvedge-to-selvedge strips.
15. With the grain line along the cut edge of the fabric, place template O3CT on the fabric strip. (See 5.19 and Helpful Hint)
16. Repeat until you have eight triangles for every octagon piece.

Fussy-cut triangles

1. To make fussy-cut triangles, trace template O3CT onto template plastic.
2. Use the seam lines as a guide when finding a motif on your fabric. When you find a pleasing area outlined by the triangle, mark the template with an outline of a prominent part of the pattern.
3. Cut out eight identical triangles from the same part of the pattern.
4. Arrange the triangles in a pleasing pattern so that all the center points are the same motif.

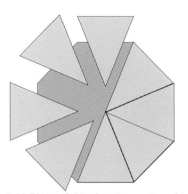

5.20 Place eight triangles on top of an octagonal piece with the right sides together and the grain line of the triangles along the cut edge of the octagon.

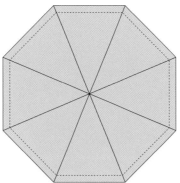

5.21 Join the triangles to the octagon by sewing around the eight sides.

5.22 Place star-shaped piece onto the fabric, right sides together, rotating the star so all edges are on the bias. Sew along all edges.

Construction

1. Place eight triangles on top of an octagonal piece with the right sides together and the grain line of the triangles along the cut edge of the octagon. Note: You may ignore the grain line for fussy-cut triangles. (See 5.20)
2. Join the triangles to the octagon by sewing ¼-inch from the edge around all eight sides. (See 5.21)
3. Trim the seam to approximately ⅛-inch along the sides of the octagon.
4. Press the triangles open with the seam allowance toward the triangles. This forms an eight-pointed star.
5. Place this star-shaped piece onto the 21-inch fabric square, right sides together, rotating the star so all edges are on the bias. Pin at the points to secure the bias edges.
6. Sew along all the edges of the pieced-star, making the inner corner turns at the dots marked on the octagon piece. Cross the stitching at the points. (See 5.22)
7. Using scissors, cut out the star-shaped piece ⅛-inch from the seam line, being careful not to get too close to the stitching.
8. Trim the outside points and clip the inside corners to ease the turning.

Batting

1. Photocopy the O3C template made earlier and cut it inside the dotted line.
2. With the batting out of the package, unfold it carefully.
3. Refold it into four smooth layers.
4. Cut a strip of batting the same width as the batting template – approximately 9¼ inches.
5. Place the batting template on the strip.
6. Place a rotary ruler on the template and line up the edge of the ruler with the edge of the template. Cut through four layers of batting.
7. Repeat until you have the number of batting pieces needed.

Attaching the batting

In Version One, the backside of the unit will be the whole star-shaped piece. In Version Two, the octagon piece is the back of the unit.

1. Fuse a piece of batting to the fabric that will form the backside of the unit by pressing or by spraying it with temporary adhesive.
2. Align the piece of batting so that it is centered.

Helpful Hint

◆◆◆

In step 6 of "Construction," it's a good idea to shorten your machine's stitch length around the outside of the points and at the inside of the corners. These areas will be trimmed quite close, and the shorter stitches will keep them from pulling out when turned.

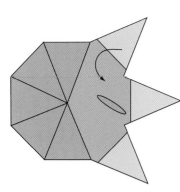

5.23 Fold the eight points to the center so that the triangles lie flat and the points meet without gaps in this Version One octagon.

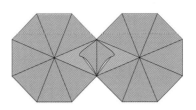

5.24 Join the pieces.

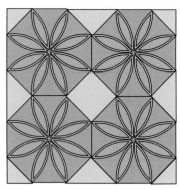

5.25 When the joining is complete, bind if desired, and turn back the petal areas.

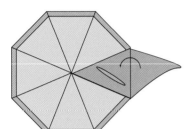

5.26 Press the folded points to complete a Version Two octagon.

Cutting the slash (Version One)

For Version One, the slash is cut in the octagon piece. For Version Two, cut the slash in the center area of the whole star-shaped piece in the center area. In both cases, this is the fabric without the batting attached.

1. Before cutting, fold a point over the area to be sure that a folded petal will cover the slash. Refer to the "Slash" section of Chapter One, page 18.
2. Cut the slash on the bias in the octagon-shaped piece. (See 5.23 for a suggested location.)
3. Turn the piece right-side out by gently pulling the fabric through the slash. Pay special attention to the corners so that all the fabric is turned to the seam allowance.
4. Press the star shape flat, making sure the seam allowances are fully open. A mini-iron is helpful with this step.
5. Fold the eight points to the center so that the triangles lie flat and the points meet without gaps. (See 5.23)
6. Press.
7. Prepare the remaining octagons in the same manner.
8. Once all are complete, prepare center squares and side-filler triangles per the instructions in the "Basic Octagon" section of this chapter, page 77.
9. Arrange the pieces according to the instructions in the project or to your own plan.
10. Join the pieces. Refer to "Joining" section in Chapter One, beginning on page 16. (See 5.24)
11. When the joining is complete, bind if desired. For Version Two projects, the outlined octagons can be left unbound, but secure the joined pieces carefully with backstitches at the outside joints.
12. Turn back the petal areas. (See 5.25)

Cutting the slash (Version Two)

1. Before cutting, check the slash location so that the folded petal will completely cover it.
2. Cut the slash on the bias in the center area of the star-shaped inner fabric piece. (Refer to 5.26 for a suggested location.)
3. Repeat steps 3, 4, and 5 of Version One.
4. Press the folded points to complete a Version Two octagon. (See 5.26)
5. Prepare the remaining octagons in the same manner.
6. Follow Version One steps 8 through 12 to complete this version.

You can dream up a number of variations to the "Accented-Petal Octagon" design, as evidenced by the three "Dreaming In Flowers" designs. Two are shown here, "Dreaming in Flowers I" (above) and "Dreaming in Flowers II" (below). Directions for these projects and a third variation follow on the next two pages.

Dreaming in Flowers
I, II & III
Accented-Petal Octagon

(Version Two)

Finished size: 17½ inches square
Difficulty level: Advanced
Block size: 8¾ inches square

Each color selection reminds me of a different time of the year: rich reds for Valentine's Day, white for summer, and dusty rose for fall. These three projects are a study in background color.

The triangles in all three projects are cut from the same floral fabric. Just the backgrounds have been changed!

These also would look pretty using a tiny, multicolored, flowered print.

Fabric requirements

Floral	1½ yards for three four-block projects
Inside/filler piece	1⅓ yards for each project
Burgundy back	⅓-yard for each project
Batting	⅓-yard of 45 inches wide

Templates

O3C	Large octagon	Two copies
O3CT	Octagon triangle	One copy

Cutting plan for each project

Floral	Four sets of eight fussy-cut triangles
Inside	Four 21-inch squares
Filler pieces	Two 4½-inch squares
	Four 4½-inch squares for triangles
Burgundy	Four octagons
Batting	Four octagons

Note how the cream-colored background makes the flower shapes fade away in this variation, "Dreaming In Flowers III."

Specific instructions

1. Follow the instructions in the "Accented-Petal Octagon" section of Chapter Five, page 91. Pay particular attention to the "Fussy-cut triangles" section.
2. Prepare four Version Two octagons, one filler square, and four filler triangles. The filler pieces in this project are made like little pillows.
3. Save your batting cutoffs from the large octagons and use them to fill the triangles.
4. Arrange the pieces and join.
5. Fold back and topstitch the petal areas. (This project is not bound.)

Helpful Hint

♦♦♦

When constructing four-part octagons, be sure to read through all the modifications before beginning.

Four-Part Octagons

The "Four-Part Octagon" pattern gives you the greatest flexibility for color choice and placement.

Because each part of the flower is a different color, very exciting effects are possible. You can choose to make subtle shades for the outlines or stark contrast for bright and dramatic looks. You can use just two triangle colors and two octagon colors for allover consistency. It's the ultimate for a leaded-glass effect, as every area is outlined. You may choose to mix up the inside octagon colors to vary the flower effects, or as with all the other techniques, mix and match all parts. The results will be very interesting!

Note how the dark green petal edges stand out against the red background and the outer edge is defined by the second red print in the "Holly Berry Petals" project, pages 100 and 101.

The technique for making these units is very similar to the "Accented-Petal Octagon." In this case, two pieced-stars are sewn together. There is an inside pieced-star and an outside pieced-star. Both are made by sewing eight triangles to a center octagon.

The inside triangles are the turn-back part of the flower petal. The inside octagon will show as the center of the petals.

The octagonal part of the outside pieced-star shows as the backside of the project and the outline at the edge of the octagon.

The triangles sewn to it are folded toward the front and form the background for the flower.

Special instructions

Follow the instructions for "Accented-Petal Octagons" in the previous section of this chapter, page 91, with the following modifications:

1. Choose four fabrics. The inner octagon is the petal-reveal. The inner triangle fabric forms the petal-accent. The front triangle fabric surrounds the petals, and the backside fabric outlines the outer edge of the front.

2. Using photocopied templates O3C (two halves taped together) and O3CT, cut each fabric into the shape designated for its position in the octagon. For each unit, you will need one inner and one outer octagon and eight each of the inner and outer triangles.

3. Mark dots through the holes in the template at the corners on the inside surface of the inner octagon.

4. Sort your inner and outer octagons and triangles into groups. If you are using several fabrics in more than one position, label which fabric goes where.

5. Skip the step that prepares the 21-inch outer squares.

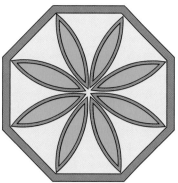

5.27 With right sides together, place an inside star on an outside star.

5.28 Join the units together and add a border or binding. Turn back the petals and topstitch.

Construction

1. Prepare an inner star-shaped unit. Following the instructions in the "Accented-Petal" section, page 91, construct an inner star from the inner octagon and eight inner triangles.
2. Press the seam allowance toward the octagon.
3. Prepare an outer star-shaped unit. Place eight outer triangles around an outer octagon piece with the right sides together and the grain line of the triangles along the cut edges of the octagon. (See 5.20, page 93.)
4. After sewing and trimming the triangles, press the seam allowance toward the triangles. This is opposite from the inner-pieced star. In the next step, these seams will lie flat against one another.
5. With right sides together, place an inside star on an outside star. (See 5.27)
6. Match the triangles at the points and at the seam allowances that were pressed in opposite directions. Pin at the points to secure the bias edges.
7. Sew along all the outside edges of the pieced-star, making the inner corner turns at the dots marked on the octagon and crossing the stitching at the points.
8. Trim around the sides of the joined star-shaped pieces to approximately ⅛-inch, being careful not to get too close to the stitching.
9. Trim the outside points and clip the inside corners to ease the turning.

Batting

1. Follow the batting instructions for star-shaped pieces in the "Batting" section of Chapter One, page 12.
2. Attach the batting octagon to the inside surface of the outer octagon fabric piece.
3. Cut the slash in the inner octagon at a point that will be covered by a folded petal flap.
4. Continue with the turning, pressing, and folding of the octagon unit.
5. Prepare filler units as needed by following the instructions in either or both of the "Filler Piece" sections of the "Basic Octagon" section of this chapter, page 80.

Assembly

1. Arrange the pieces according to the project or your own design.
2. Join the units and add a border or binding per the instructions in Chapter One, pages 14 and 12.
3. Turn back and topstitch petals. (See 5.28)
   This unit has two looks depending on which fabrics are folded to the inside.

Holly Berry Petals
Four-Part Octagon

Finished size: 18 inches square
Difficulty level: Intermediate
Block size: 9-inch octagon

Rosy red accents give this floral fabric holiday cheer. Make it as a wall or door hanging or convert it into a pillow.

The four-color octagon pattern allows you to have each part of the block in the color you choose. The background outline and the inner petals in this project are the same rosy fabric. The visual illusion ties these areas together.

Fabric requirements

Front triangles	⅓-yard floral
Background	½-yard white on white
Backing	½-yard muslin
Inside petals/back	½-yard rosy red
Border and accent	½-yard green
Binding	4 inches (included in inside petals)
Batting	18 inches square

Templates

O3C	Octagon	Two copies
O3CT	Triangle	One copy

Cutting plan

Floral	Eight outer triangles
Muslin	One 18-inch square
Rosy red	Two octagons: one inner, one outer; Two 1¾-inch strips
Green	Eight inner triangles; Two 3-inch strips
White	One 13½-inch square
Batting	One 18-inch square

Specific instructions

1. Follow the instructions in the "Four-Part Octagon" section of Chapter Five, page 98, to make the center block.
2. Complete the petal turn-back and topstitching steps.
3. Sew the 3-inch green strips to the 13½-inch white print square.
4. With right sides together, place a green strip along one edge and sew.
5. Trim the extra fabric from the strip even with the edge of the square.
6. Repeat on the opposite side of the square.
7. Open the strips and press the seam allowance toward the green strips.
8. Sew the second strip along one of the remaining sides across both green strips.
9. Trim.
10. Repeat for the last side.

Deck your halls with "Holly Berry Petals," made above by Laura Farson, for a splash of holiday good cheer.

11. Open the green strips and press the seam allowance toward the green strip.
12. Place the octagon on the center of the white print square. Find the center by folding in half both directions and finger-pressing the folds along the edge of the white square.
13. Line up the petals with the finger-pressed folds.
14. Spray-baste the block onto the fabric or pin at the corners.
15. Turn the pieces over and layer the 18-inch piece of batting on top of the backside.
16. Cut out and remove the batting behind the octagon.
17. Layer the muslin over the batting.
18. Spray-fuse or press-fuse the batting and muslin backing. If using temporary adhesive spray, just lift the batting and spritz with a little spray to keep it in place. Do the same for the muslin layer.
19. Turn the layered group to the front.
20. Topstitch along the outer edge of the block with monofilament thread. (I use the hemstitch with a narrow width.)
21. Sew a straight stitch with the monofilament thread through all layers around the inside edge of the border.
22. Bind with the two 1¾-inch rosy red strips.

Hanging option

1. From cutoffs, fold three strips of 6-inch-long fabric so that all the raw edges are inside.
2. Topstitch.
3. Fold each of the three strips in the center.
4. Pin one of the strips to each of the upper corners of the square and one in the center.
5. Tack with a few stitches.
6. Place a rod through the loops to hang the project.

6 dodecagons

Chapter Guide
Dodecagon Techniques
◆ Basic Dodecagon,
   page 103

*I*t's difficult to pick a favorite, but the sunflower design vies for mine! Inspired by the lush yellow fields of Kansas, it's hard to resist.

The sunflower, with its twelve sides, is called a "dodecagon."

Once you get past the odd name, you realize that they can look great in quilting projects as yellow sunflowers, creamy daisies, and red poinsettias.

Thus, color choice determines the desired flower outcome. The dramatic contrast of green and yellow, enhanced by shading, in "Sunny Days in Kansas" (page 109) gives a very summery appearance. Deep rich reds opposite leafy green create the impression of Christmas. For spring, choose light yellow, pale grassy green, and white on white for a crisp, clean look.

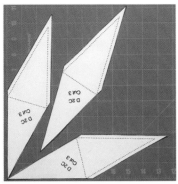

6.1 Matching the centers, arrange the template pieces as shown here.

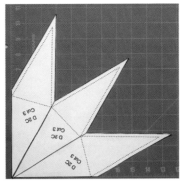

6.2 Tape the three diamonds together to form a quarter of a star-shaped template.

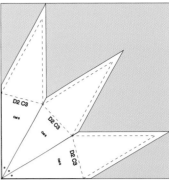

6.3 Place the template on the fabric, matching the inside corner to the folds.

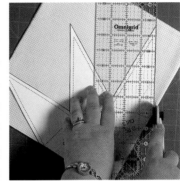

6.4 Place a rotary-cutting ruler on top of the template.

Basic Dodecagons

Although a twelve-sided shape can appear a bit daunting, the extra effort in constructing this variation yields a beautiful flower blossom with twelve petals.

Preparing the template

1. Photocopy template D2C3 on page 126 three times.
2. Cut along the solid lines on all copies.
3. Matching the centers, arrange the template pieces, first with two outside star points and then inserting the third piece between the two. (See 6.1)
4. Tape the three diamonds together to form a quarter of a star-shaped template. It is helpful to align the two outside pieces, using removable tape, on your cutting mat lines so that they are at right angles. (See 6.2)

Construction

1. Organize your fabric choices into a group for the inside pieces and one for the outside.
2. After folding the fabric selvedge to selvedge, cut 22-inch lengths from both the front and back fabrics. Cut the length in half to make a roughly 22- by 22-inch square.
3. Fold one piece of the inside fabric two times to form a "square." Be sure that the raw edges are exactly even. Press each fold as you make it.
4. Spray the backside of the paper template with temporary adhesive spray.
5. Place the template on the fabric, matching the inside corner to the folds. (See 6.3)
6. Place a rotary-cutting ruler on top of the template, lining up the ¼-inch line with the dotted line of the template. (See 6.4)
7. Cut through four layers of fabric along the edge of the ruler with a rotary cutter.
8. Repeat along the outside lines, outlining the points. Do not cut on the fold lines.
9. Remove the template and unfold the fabric. You should have a star with twelve points.
10. Press.
11. Place this star-shaped fabric piece, with right sides together, on a 22-inch square of the background fabric. Avoid aligning the straight edges of the star along the grain line of the back fabric so that all the angles fall on the bias. (See 6.5)
12. Pin the points to the inside piece to secure the bias edges.
13. Sew along all star points ¼-inch from the edges, crossing the stitching. Use a walking foot to keep the edges flat. (See Helpful Hint)

Helpful Hint

◆◆◆

If you have a tie-down feature on your sewing machine, it's helpful to use it at both the inside and outside corners. Otherwise, decrease stitch length in the corners and at the points.

6.5 Place this star-shaped fabric piece, right-side down on a 22-inch square of the background fabric.

Helpful Hint

♦♦♦

After step 14 of "Construction," remind yourself which fabric is for the outside and which is for the inside. This is very important when using multiple fabrics.

6.6 Trim the seam allowance back to 1/8-inch, being very careful not to get too close to the stitching.

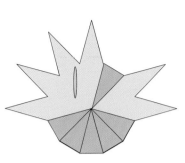

6.7 Turn the piece right-side out by gently pulling the fabric through the slash.

14. Trim the seam allowance back to approximately ⅛-inch, being very careful not to get too close to the stitching. Snip across the outside corners and at an angle to smooth them. Make a clip and trim at an angle into the inside corners to ease the turning. (See 6.6 and Helpful Hint)
15. With the inner fabric facing up, cut a slash 2 inches long through just one layer across the bias in the center area of the star-shaped piece.
16. Locate the slash so that it will be hidden under a folded petal flap.
17. Lift a single layer of fabric at about the center of where you would like the slash.
18. Pinch it into a tiny fold and snip across the fold. Be sure you only have one layer of fabric!
19. Then insert your scissors into the snip and cut first 1 inch in one direction and then an inch in the opposite. Cutting across the bias keeps the slash from fraying.

Batting

If batting is desired, the lightest/thinnest ("Gold Fuse" or Thermore) works best, as there are many layers of fabric close together in this design.

1. Cut batting pieces using a paper template cut ¼-inch smaller than the center dodecagon.
2. Create the template by tracing around an unturned, folded unit and cutting it ¼-inch smaller. To do this, fold the points to the center of an unturned unit.
3. Place on a piece of paper and trace around it.
4. Place the ¼-inch line of a rotary ruler on the line so that the ¼-inch line is on the inside of the traced dodecagon.
5. Draw a line.
6. Repeat for the twelve sides.
7. Cut on the inside lines.
8. Carefully unfold the batting.
9. Refold it two times creating four smoothed layers.
10. With a large rotary ruler and cutter, cut a strip the width of the batting template.
11. Place the template on the batting strip with a rotary ruler along the edge.
12. Cut along the ruler with a rotary cutter. Save the cutoffs to use later for the middle filler pieces.
13. Spray-fuse or press-fuse the batting to the center of the wrong side of the outside fabric.
14. Turn the piece right-side out by gently pulling the fabric through the slash. Pay special attention to the points so that all the fabric is turned to the seam allowance. (See 6.7)
15. Press the star shape flat, making sure the seam allowances are fully open.
16. Fold the points to the center to form a dodecagon (twelve-sided figure).

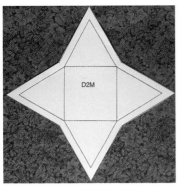

6.8 Photocopy template D2M, cut along the solid lines, and use it to cut the front fabric.

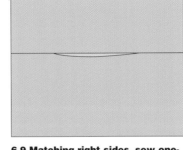

6.9 Matching right sides, sew one-third of the seam, back-tack, skip one-third, back-tack, and finish.

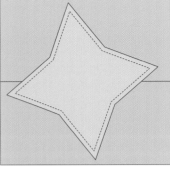

6.10 Place a front unit on the back square with right sides together, alingned so the opening doesn't intersect with the points of the star.

17. Align the points so that the corners lie flat. Press.

18. Prepare the remaining stars in the same manner.

19. Once the dodecagons are complete, prepare the filler units.

Filler units

Filler units are made two ways.

When a whole center unit is needed, as in the situation where four flowers meet, the filler unit is made with an opening used to turn it right-side out.

Because side- and corner-filler units can be cut in half or fourths before turning, they don't need an opening. The two methods are explained here.

Whole center filler unit

The front fabric of a center unit is cut with a template into a star shape. This star is placed right-side down on a square that has been seamed to provide an opening for turning. Batting is fused to the wrong side of the front fabric, and the unit is turned to the right side through the opening in the back piece.

1. Photocopy the star-shaped template labeled D2M, page 127, and cut it along the solid lines.

2. Cut front fabric using the D2M template. (See 6.8)

3. Cut back fabric into 10-inch squares. Cut the squares in half one time.

4. Matching the right sides, sew the square halves together along the long side as follows: sew one-third of the seam, back-tack, skip one-third of the seam, back-tack, and finish the seam. (See 6.9)

5. Open flat and press the seam allowance to one side. The skipped area becomes a finished-edged opening that will be used later to flip the unit to the right side.

6. Place a front unit on the back square with right sides together and aligned so that the opening doesn't intersect with the points of the star. In other words, offset the star so that the seam is below or above the points. (See 6.10)

7. Sew ⅛-inch around the edge of the star-shaped front unit.

8. Cut out the star-shaped piece ⅛-inch from the stitching, trim the points, and clip the inner corners.

9. Cut a piece of batting ½-inch smaller than the sewn unit or use the cutoffs from the large center batting pieces.

10. Place the pieces on the wrong side of the front fabric to arrange them before fusing. (See 6.11)

11. Spray-fuse or press-fuse the batting pieces to the wrong side of the front fabric.

12. Turn the piece right-side out by gently pulling the fabric through the opening in the seam of the back piece. Pay special attention to the points so that the fabric is fully turned to the seam allowance.

13. Sew some quilting lines in the center to close the opening, and press.

6.11 Place batting pieces on wrong side of the front fabric and arrange them before fusing. Then, spray-fuse or press-fuse.

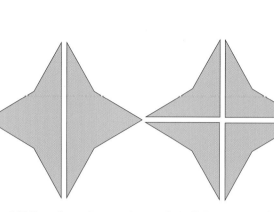

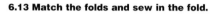

6.12 For edge units, cut the star in half. For corner units, cut again perpendicular to first cut.

6.13 Match the folds and sew in the fold.

Edge and corner units

Edge and corner units are made using the D2M template on page 127. The finished opening is not necessary because the whole pieces are cut in half. The star-shaped front fabric is sewn to a back square. Once the batting is fused onto it, it is cut into smaller pieces. Then, it is turned right-side out.

1. Cut front fabric using the D2M template.
2. Cut back fabric into 7-inch squares.
3. Place a front piece on a back square with right sides together, pin, and sew ⅛-inch seam around the outside.
4. Trim away any extra fabric ⅛-inch from the stitching line.
5. Spray-baste a piece, or pieces, of batting to the wrong side of the outside fabric. These batting pieces are also the same size as the cutoffs of the larger piece.
6. For edge units, cut the star in half with the ruler placed from point to point through the middle of the star. For the corner units, cut again perpendicular to the first cut. (See 6.12)
7. Flip the pieces to their right sides.
8. Be sure to fully open the seam allowances and press flat.

Joining

1. Arrange the units as shown in the project or in your own pattern.
2. Once the arrangement is complete, sew the units together. (It is easier to join the horizontal seams first, creating vertical strips.)
3. Open the folded points of two touching flower units.
4. Match the folds and sew in the fold. (See 6.13)
5. Return the petal flaps to their folded position and pin in place.
6. Once all the horizontal seams are sewn together, repeat with the vertical

6.14 Place a center connector unit over each space, with the seam opening facing up on the backside.

6.15 Once turned over to the front side, you can see how nicely the units are aligned.

6.16 Open the petal flaps and pin across the flap folds. Remove tape and sew along the fold lines and through the filler unit.

seams.

7. There will be large spaces between the dodecagon units.
8. Turn the joined units over to the back.
9. Place a center filler unit over each of these spaces with the seam opening facing up on the backside. Make sure that the middle unit is centered by lining up the corners of the star with the joining seams of the flower units. (See 6.14 and Helpful Hint)
10. Turn the units over to the front side. (See 6.15)
11. Open the petal flaps of the flower units that lie over the filler piece and pin across the fold of the flaps. Remove the tape, as it will gum up the sewing machine needle. (See 6.16)
12. Sew along the fold lines and through the filler unit, being careful not to catch the petal flaps in the seam.
13. Return the flaps to their original folded positions and pin at their centers.
14. Repeat for each of the center units and then for any edge-filler units.

Finishing

1. Add a border and/or bind, as instructed on pages 14 and 12 of Chapter One.
2. Finish by topstitching the petal flaps. Refer to the "Turning Back Petals" section of Chapter One, page 20. (See 6.17)

Helpful Hint

♦♦♦

I usually secure the center units in place with masking tape along the outside edges.

6.17 The finished quilt will look like this.

Sunny Days in Kansas
Two-Color Dodecagon

This quilt was inspired by a drive across Kansas in late-summer, when the sunflower fields were laden with blooms. Mix and match shades of gold, yellow, and green.

Finished size: 40 inches square
Difficulty level: Advanced
Block size: 10 inches square

Fabric requirements

Yellow/gold	1¼ yards of four shades
Green	1¼ yards of four shades
Dark green	2 yards (⅓-yard binding; 1⅔ yards filler pieces)
Batting	1½ yards of 45 inches wide

Templates

D2C3	Dodecagon	Three copies
D2M	Filler-star piece	One copy

Cutting plan

Green	Sixteen 21-inch squares (four of each shade)
Yellow	Sixteen 21-inch squares folded and cut into dodecagon stars
Dark green	Five 1¾-inch strips binding
	Nine 9- by 10-inch rectangles for filler stars with turning slots
	Seven 7-inch squares for cut filler stars
Sixteen filler stars	
Batting	Sixteen small dodecagons
	Sixteen filler stars (can use cutoffs from dodecagon)

Specific instructions

1. Follow the instructions in Chapter Six for dodecagons, page 103.
2. Prepare sixteen dodecagons, nine whole filler stars with turning slots, and seven filler stars to be divided as follows.
3. Cut six stars in half. Cut the seventh one twice to make four corner pieces.
4. Arrange the parts as shown in the photo.
5. Join the pieces in rows.
6. Join rows into pairs and then join the two pairs.
7. Although it is more awkward, turn back the petals and topstitch after you bind the quilt.

A drive through the bloom-laden coutryside can inspire the clever quilter. Such was the case for this 40-inch square quilt, "Sunny Days in Kansas," made by Laura Farson, 2001.

Navy Blues Pillow
Two-Color Dodecagon

Finished size: 18 inches square
Difficulty level: Intermediate
Block size: 10-inch dodecagon

If joining unit after unit for an entire quilt seems too daunting or is going to take more time than you have planned for, just use a single unit for a smaller project—like a pillow!

Make this tailored-looking pillow for a formal living room. Its simplicity of color lends itself to blend in with a cream-colored sofa or chair.

Fabric requirements

Inside	⅔-yard cream print
Outside	⅔-yard navy print
Background	½-yard cream figure
Backing	½-yard muslin
Border	½-yard navy dot
Back side	½-yard plain navy
Batting	18 inches square
Pillow form	16 inches square

Templates

D2C3	Dodecagon	Three copies

Cutting plan

Cream print	One 22-inch square cut into one dodecagon star
Navy print	One 22-inch square
Cream figure	One 14-inch square
Navy dot	Two 3-inch strips
Navy solid	Two 12½- by 18-inch rectangles
Muslin	One 18-inch square

Specific instructions

1. Follow the instructions in Chapter Six to make the center dodecagon block, page 103.
2. Complete the petal turn-back and topstitching steps.
3. Sew the 3-inch navy-dotted strips to the 14-inch white-print square.
4. With right sides together, place a navy strip along one edge and sew.

A single flower unit can be used all on its own, as was the case here in "Navy Blues Pillow," made by Laura Farson, 2001.

5. Trim the extra fabric from the strip even with the edge of the square.
6. Repeat on the opposite side of the square.
7. Open the strips and press the seam allowance toward the navy.
8. Sew the second strip along one of the remaining sides across both navy strips.
9. Trim.
10. Repeat for the last side.

Continued on next page.

Helpful Hint

◆◆◆

If using temporary
adhesive spray, just lift
the batting and spritz
with a little spray to keep
it in place. Do the same
for the muslin layer.

Navy Blues Pillow continued

11. Open the seams.

12. Press the seam allowance toward the navy.

13. Place the octagon on the center of the white print square. Find the center by folding in half in both directions and finger-pressing the folds along the edge of the white square.

14. Line up the petals with the finger-pressed folds.

15. Spray-baste the block onto the fabric or pin at the corners.

16. Turn the pieces over and layer the 18-inch piece of batting on top of the backside.

17. Cut out and remove the batting behind the dodecagon.

18. Layer the muslin over the batting.

19. Spray-fuse or press-fuse the batting and muslin backing. (See Helpful Hint)

20. Turn the layered group to the front. Topstitch along the outer edge of the block with monofilament thread. (I use the hemstitch with a narrow width.)

21. Sew a straight stitch with monofilament thread through all layers around the inside edge of the border.

22. The backside of the pillow has a slotted opening for ease of turning now and for changing or laundering later. Prepare the back piece by folding over 2 inches on the long side of one of the navy rectangles.

23. Topstitch along this raw edge of the turned piece. The piece now measures 10½ by 18 inches.

24. With right sides facing each other, place the hemmed piece on the front square so that the raw edges are matched.

25. Lay the unhemmed piece on top of the hemmed piece so that its center over-laps about 4½ inches and its edges line up with the other end of the front square. Sew around all the edges.

26. Trim the corners and flip to the outside through the slot in the navy square.

27. Insert the 16-inch pillow form into the slot and smooth the front so that it is unwrinkled.

A Final Word

I hope you've enjoyed the techniques and projects presented here. I also hope they've inspired your imagination and creativity!

Additional possibilities, such as flower collages, variations in color placement, and endless fabric choices, can be explored.

If you liked *Fast-Folded Flowers*, there's more to come. Exciting new designs and techniques are being developed. They include: unique leaf patterns, cutaway versions of hexagons and octagons, more fussy-cut pattern variations, and new petal shapes for squares. I'm looking forward to sharing them with you.

For questions, additional information, rigid plastic templates, and products, consult my Web site: www.fastfoldedflowers.com.

Templates

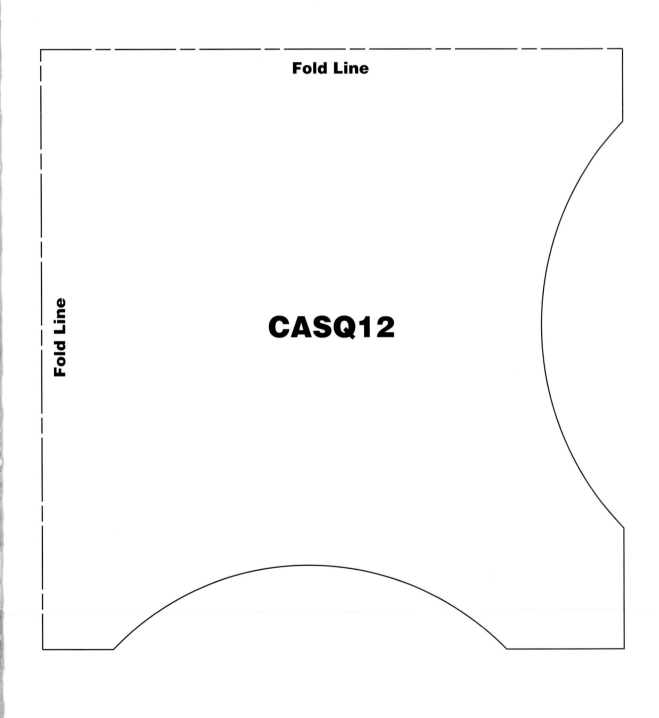

Fold Line

Fold Line

CASQ12

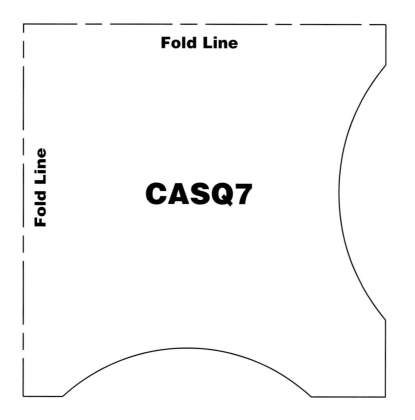

Fold Line

Fold Line

CASQ7

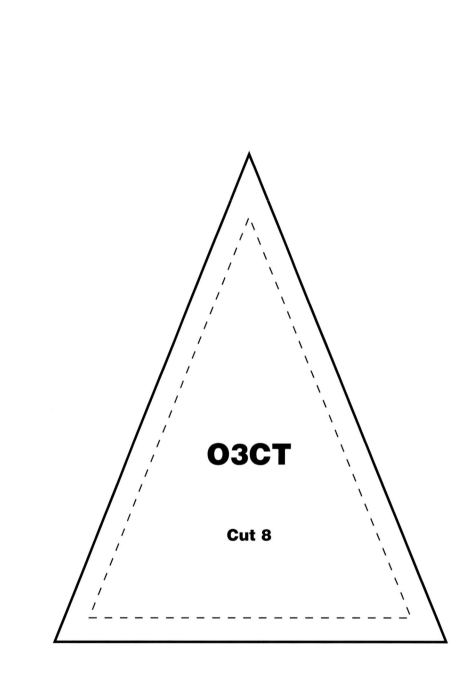

O3CT

Cut 8

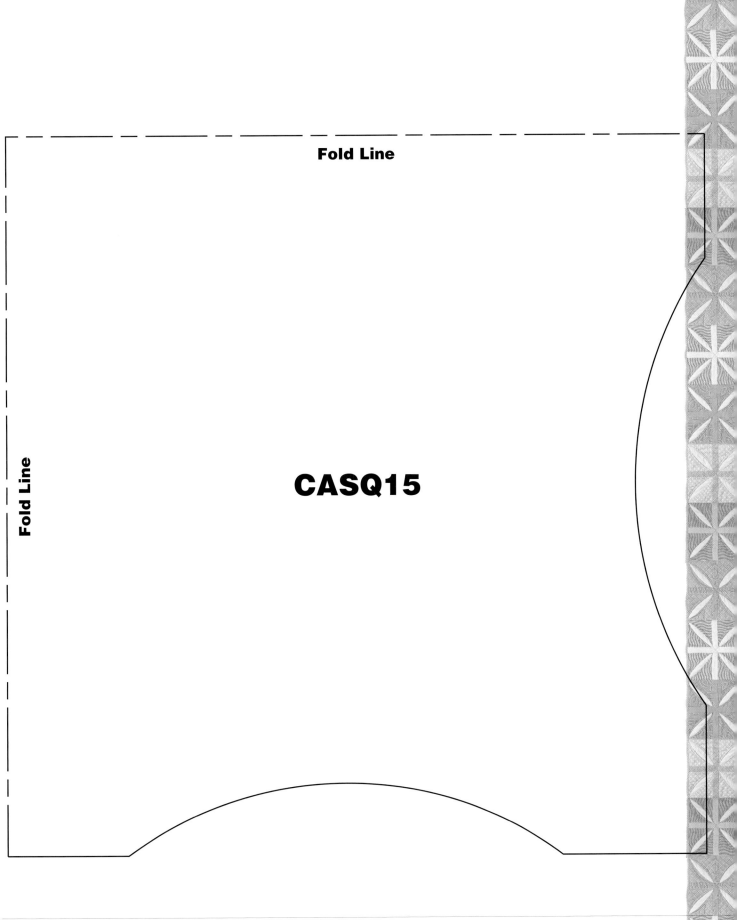

Fold Line

Fold Line

CASQ15

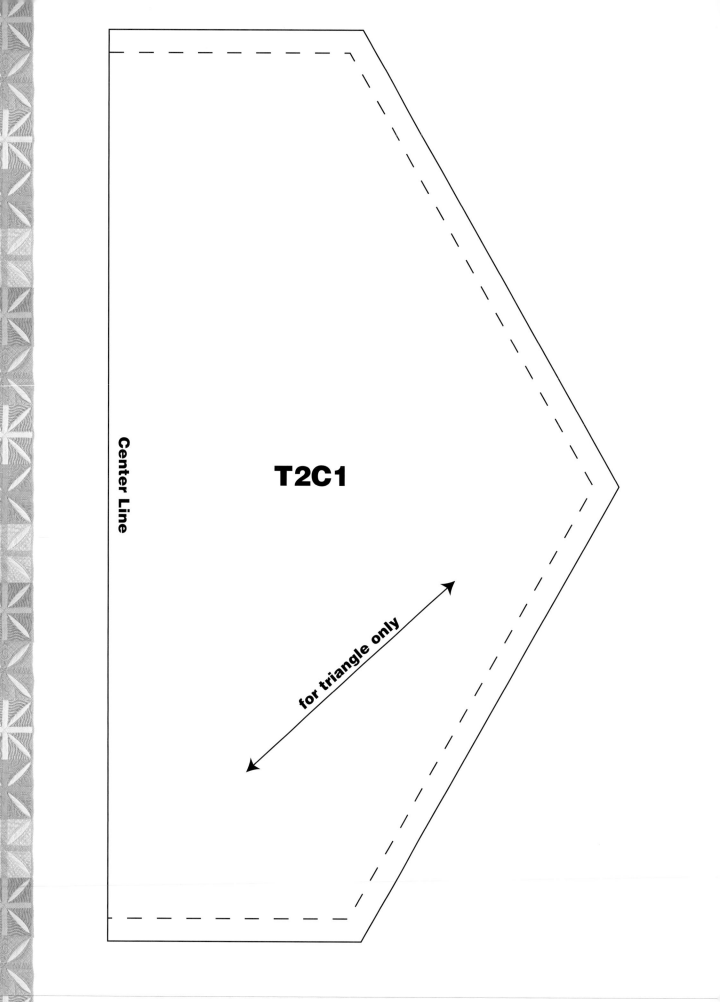

Center Line

T2C1

for triangle only

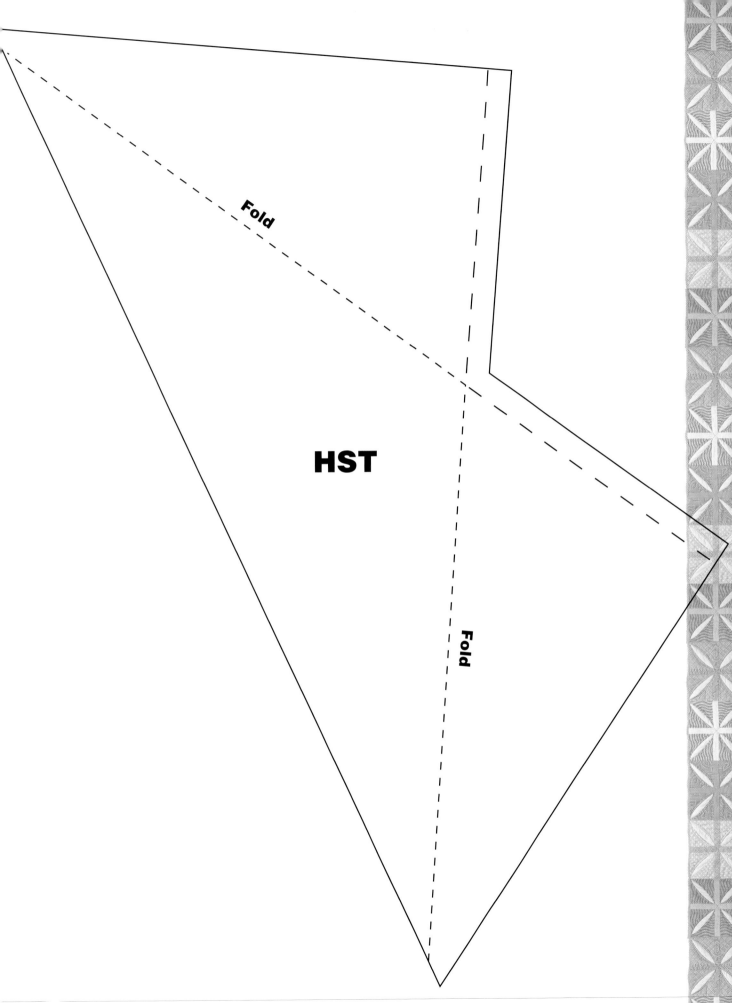

HST

Fold

Fold

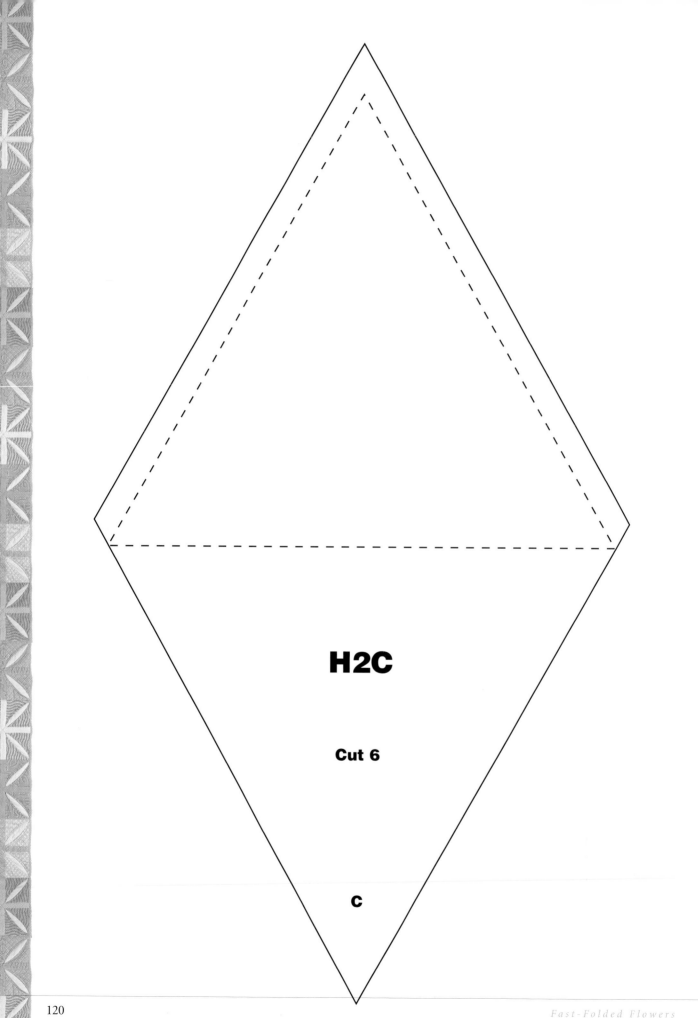

H2C

Cut 6

c

Fast-Folded Flowers

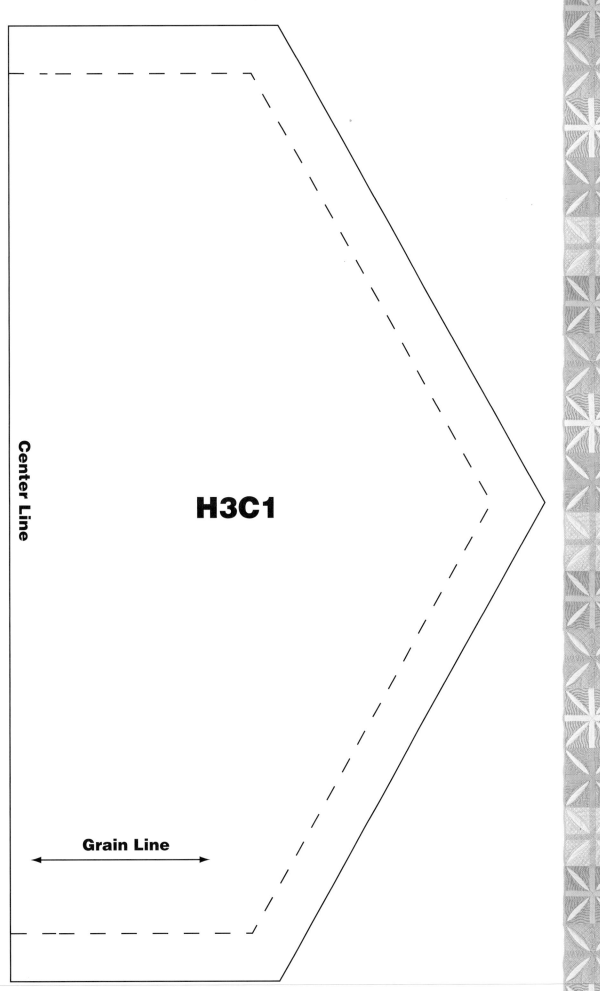

Center Line

H3C1

Grain Line

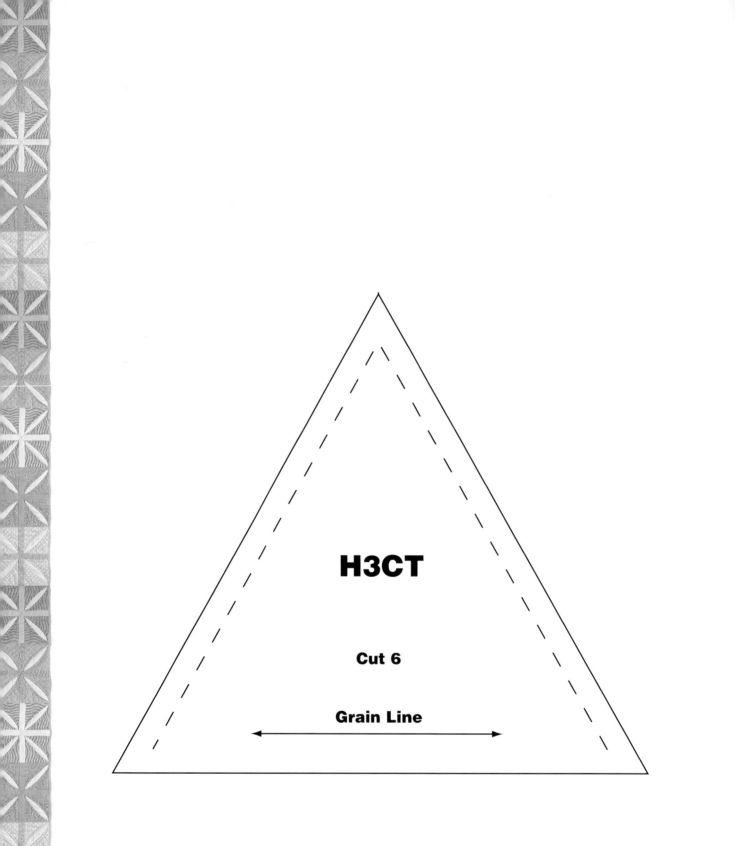

H3CT

Cut 6

Grain Line

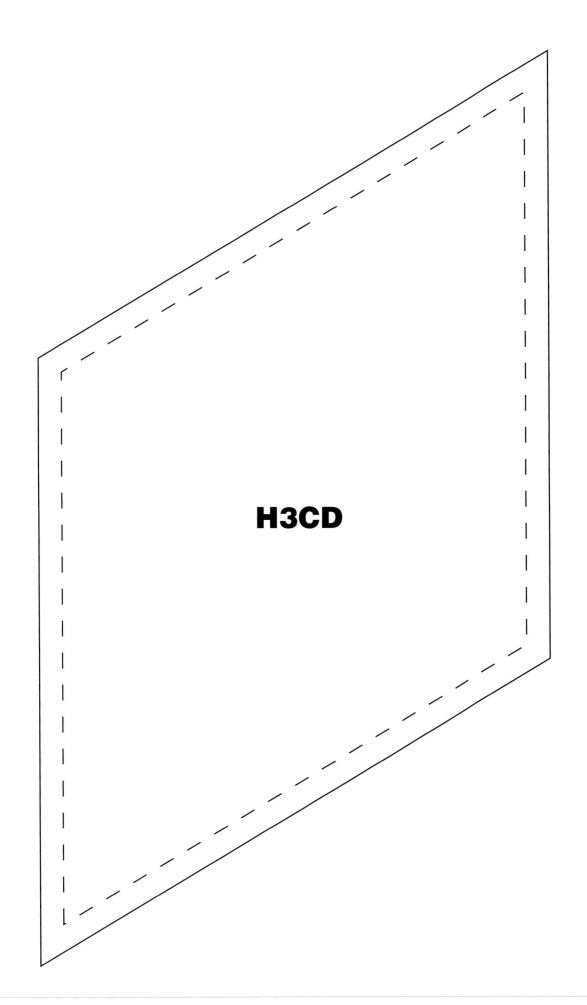

H3CD

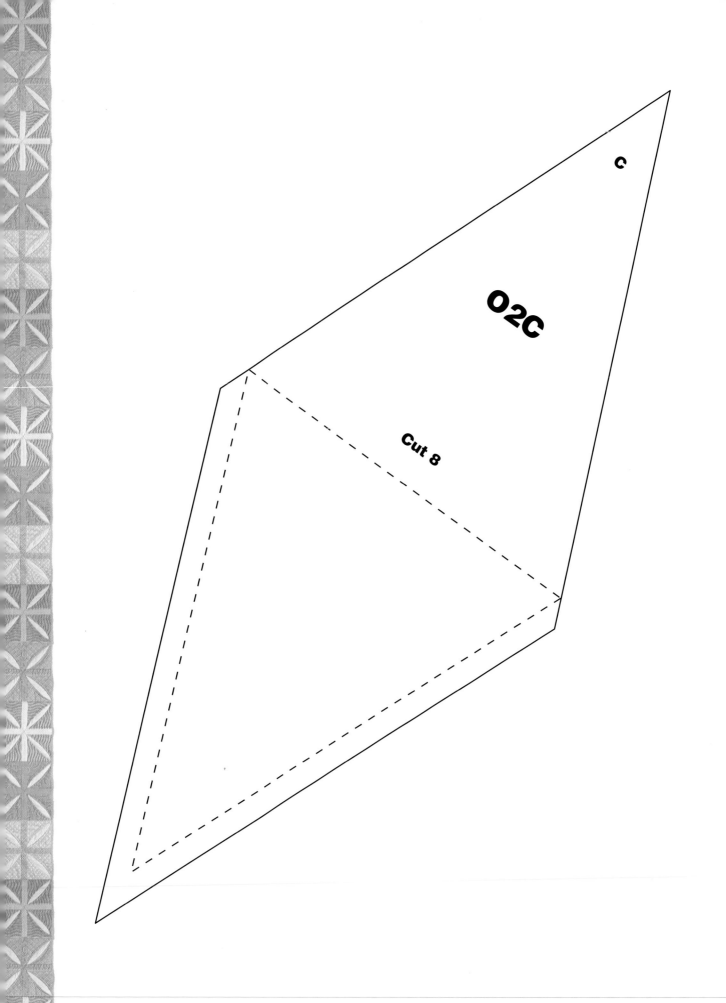

O2C

Cut 8

c

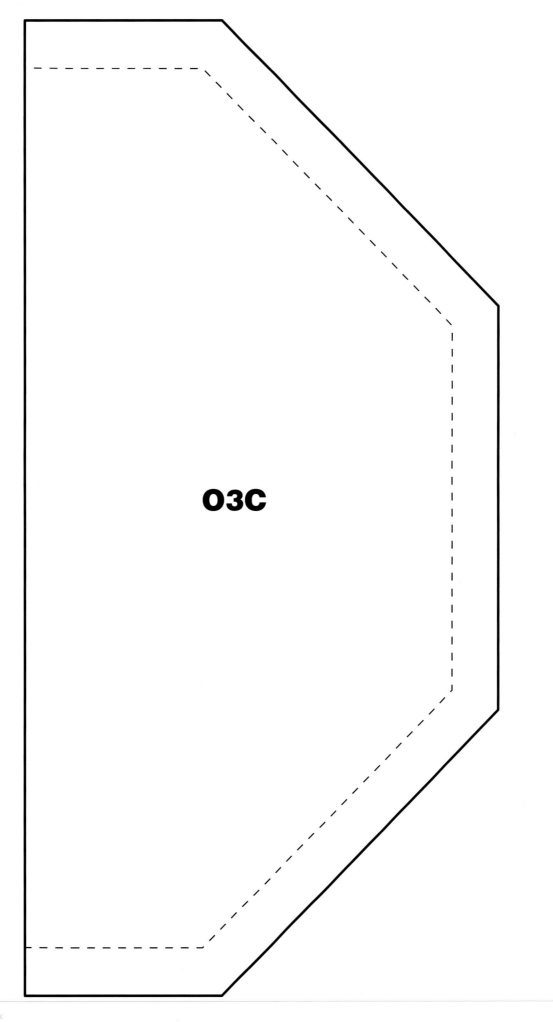

O3C

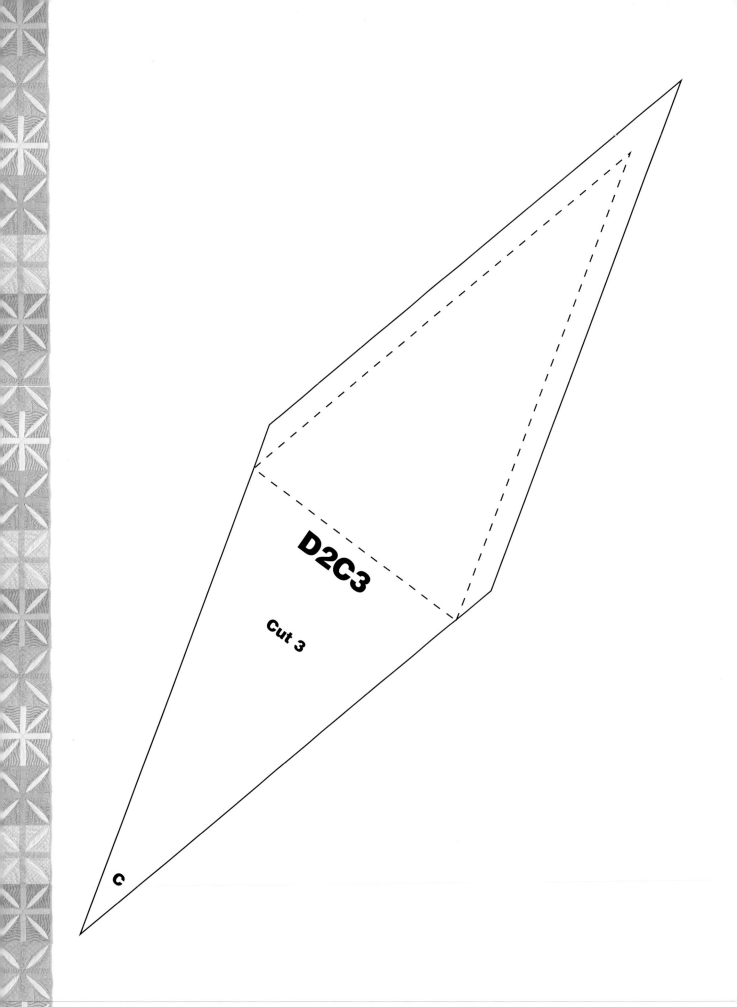

D2C3

Cut 3

C

Fast-Folded Flowers

D2M

Index